5
Days
to a New
Marriage

Terry Hargrave, Ph.D. & Shawn Stoever, Ph.D.

Five Days to a New Marriage

Published by The Hideaway Foundation
1800 S. Washington Street
Suite 215
Amarillo, Texas 79012
www.fivedaystoanewmarriage.com

Details in some anecdotes and stories have been changed to protect the identities of the persons involved.

ISBN 978-1-4276-4887-7

Library of Congress Cataloging-in-Publication Data

Published in the United States of America

2011—First Edition

10 9 8 7 6 5 4

To all the courageous couples who have worked
to create a new marriage when it seemed as though
all hope was lost.

Contents

Preface 7

1. **The Pain Cycle** 13

   Reviewing the Past to Understand the Present

2. **The Peace Cycle** 37

   Reestablishing the Truth to Get Healthy

3. **"Us-ness"** 61

   Reconnecting to the New Self and the New Relationship

4. **A Different Future** 83

   Relaunching to a New Marriage

5. **Your New Marriage—Forever** 103

   Understanding Where to Go From Here

Acknowledgments 109

Preface

"Your marriage is over."

"Your marriage cannot change."

Have you heard one of these statements echoing in your mind? If so, we're here to tell you it is a lie. It is a lie of fear that you and your identity will be stolen or, worse yet, wasted in a relationship that takes advantage of you. A lie of doubt, filling your mind with thoughts of regret that you ever chose your spouse. A lie of anger telling you that intimacy is over and the best you can tolerate is living separate lives, perhaps under the same roof.

Who tells you this lie? It certainly comes from a society that teaches that marriage is temporary and if your spouse does not make you happy, you should move on. Maybe it comes from some of your friends and family who believe that your spouse, at best, is not the right person for you or, at worst, is a jerk or a nag. It may come from yourself because you have bought into the idea that your marriage is not built to last and you hooked up with a bad person. Maybe it comes from evil spiritual forces who offer you an apparent way out at the same time they are hoping to see your destruction.

Whatever the source of the lie you are believing, we have something else to tell you, something radical and true. Your marriage can be saved and improved. And you, personally, can grow and change for the better within the context of your marriage. We are not telling you there is never a reason for divorce or you are somehow bad if you do divorce. But we are saying it is a lie that you cannot change and that your marriage is beyond hope.

You can have a new marriage with your current spouse. A better marriage—maybe even one you never imagined was possible.

For a couple of significant reasons we can tell you this remarkable truth.

First, a good God is on your side. He wants you to know that He deeply and passionately loves you, believes in your potential, and wants to see you grow and flourish to become the amazing human being that even you may doubt you are. He will use all of your relationships, especially your marriage, as a mechanism to make this happen.

Second, we have counseled hundreds of couples who came in with dead marriages. We have watched in amazement as they invested five days of dedicated energy that resulted in transformed lives and relationships.

Jim and Martha came in with one of those seemingly dead marriages.

Martha said at the start of our intensive work together, "When I was driving here, I thought to myself that it would take nothing short of a miracle to change my heart. We are so locked into the same fights and are so distant from one another that I cannot imagine ever finding our way back to actually love one another. I can't even imagine being civil to one another!"

Jim was just as adamant, if more succinct. "The marriage—what marriage?"

But after going through the *Five Days to a New Marriage* process, Jim and Martha were believers in its effectiveness.

"It is hard to believe, but a miracle has happened," Martha attested. "These are not some nice words that we speak over our marriage, but for the first time we are looking at our problems head-on and see the root of our issues. When we turned that first corner and actually were able to stay out of that old pattern of fighting, it was like I saw the man that I fell in love with years ago. We have hope that we didn't have before."

Similarly Jim said, "For the first time in our marriage, the tools make sense. We've learned lots of lists and answers, but this is the first program that is simple enough to follow but profound enough to change us and our marriage."

So here is the deal. This book is designed to help you confront some of the lies and problems driving your marriage to a desperate state or to hopeless stagnation. It is based in the belief that if you change the pattern of your interactions by listening to truths instead of lies, you can change your marriage—for good. It will give you a step-by-step, day-by-day process to help you get some important facts into your life and into your marriage relationship. If your spouse is willing to follow this process along with you, it will certainly offer more opportunity for you both to improve your marriage. But, even if he or she is unwilling, start the work by yourself; you will likely find that following the framework can cause enough change to interest your spouse in getting involved.

We have learned these truths and techniques in a variety of places, and then we have refined the process over many years in the context of intensive marital therapy. Intensive marital therapy is different from traditional therapy in that it occurs for many hours over a period of several consecutive days. It is sometimes conducted between one therapist and one couple but most often involves four couples in a group with two therapists. The particular method described in this book is the one used by The Hideaway Experience (*www.thehideawayexperience.com*) outside of Amarillo, Texas. This comfortable, sequestered setting allows couples in trouble to get away for four days, walking through a process you will soon read about, with the help of professional counselors and therapists.

The many couples who have been to The Hideaway Experience are much like you. Some are desperate and on their last hope that their marriages can change. Some are frustrated that their marriages are stuck in a place of irresolvable issues with little or no intimacy. Some are in better places with their marriages but realize something is missing, and they want their marriages to be great. And the amazing thing is that couples from all of these types of situations have been successful in changing their marriages using the *Five Days to a New Marriage* approach.

We ourselves—your authors—have had some of these same marriage issues. We have struggled, fought, cried, been corrected by our wives, and learned. We are works in progress just like everyone else. But we have found that these principles do work in our own lives and marriages.

So, no matter what the state of your marriage is, you can get better if you read the material, do the exercises, and apply the methods found here. If you are faithful to do the work, God is faithful and will honor your efforts to change.

The couples at The Hideaway are amazed that they are able to begin their new marriage in five days. We want you to have the same amazing experience. So we have arranged the material in the same kind of five-day time frame. One chapter equals one day. Of course you can take as long as you want to read the material. But if you chose to read and follow it in five days, you can see a new marriage start in as little as time as that.

Many couples will read this book as part of a small-group study over an eight-week period, coordinated with the *Five Days to a New Marriage Small-Group Leader's Guide*. If you are in one of these groups, don't get hung up about following a day-by-day format. Simply follow the instructions for reading given by the group. But whether you read and work through the book in a matter of days or weeks, what is here can change your life.

When you sit down to read, follow these simple guidelines:

1. Say a prayer to God to enlighten your reading and to bless your spouse, regardless of where he or she is physically or emotionally.

2. Read no more than one chapter per day. If you are part of a study group that moves through the material more slowly, or if you just want to take more time, it is great to read even less than one chapter per day. The main idea is not to get into a hurry with the material.

3. Work through all the exercises in each chapter as you are reading.

4. After you are finished with each chapter, review the *"Idea to Remember"* boxes.

5. Do your best, with your spouse, to practice what you have learned. It is great if your spouse will join you in reading this book, but it is best to work through the exercises on your own. After you have completed the exercises, share with your spouse what you have learned about yourself and practice together what you both have learned.

If you follow these instructions, relax and take a deep breath, then read, you will find hope and realize that change is possible.

If you are believing lies about your marriage, you can begin to live in the truth. And the truth is that your marriage can become whole through your faithful work and God's gracious care. In only five days.

6. Download to your smart phone our new app "New Marriage" and enter all your and your spouses information as you go through each of the five chapters.

The Pain Cycle

Reviewing the Past to Understand the Present

Day 1

We know that you may feel stuck, discouraged, or hopeless in your marriage. But based on our many years of experience with troubled marriages, we are confident about something else: that you can do the work outlined in this brief book and turn your marriage around. You can move out of your crisis or stagnant mode and into a vibrant and growing marriage relationship.

Maybe a nagging feeling that you don't quite understand has you and your spouse living more like roommates than partners. Maybe something big like hate, a financial disaster, or the grind of argument after argument makes you wonder if you can live together or even be in one another's presence. Regardless, you can do this work of saving your marriage.

You can do this!

But in order for you to be able to do this work, you have to face some of the issues that brought you to this place of unhappiness. It is like when you were a kid and you got a bad scrape on the playground. The wound hurt enough as it was, but if you just covered it up and didn't get it properly treated, it festered and got worse with infection or other complications. We don't want you to just cover your marital problems and issues with some easy and unrealistic solutions. We want you to take the time to examine the wound, get it cleaned up, and learn what you need to do in order to get the issue healed. That means that you need to take a good look at the past and face some of the causes that brought you to where you are today.

Many people will argue that you should never look back and that you should only be forward focused. We do think that there are some advantages to being positive and looking to what can be done in the future instead of just rehashing the past. But most of the things that we talk about in this chapter are designed to help you understand the part of your past that keeps coming up when you don't understand it and causes you to do things that you don't like about yourself. We want to review this past, understand it, and disarm it so it doesn't control your emotions and your behaviors.

IDEA To Remember:

You can do this.

Of course, an easier solution would be to say that, if your marriage is not working, you don't need to look at the past but instead look for another spouse. In other words, divorce is the answer to marital problems. Could that be right? We don't think so. And we don't think God thinks so.

God is not so much anti-divorce as He wants couples to succeed at marriage. Divorce is a violent act that tears people down and makes it more difficult for families to exist in growing, prospering relationships. As Jeremiah 29:11 says, " *'I know the plans I have for you,' declares the Lord, 'plans to prosper you and not to harm you, plans to give you hope and a future.'* " Divorce, by contrast, wreaks violence on a family. Is it any wonder, then, that God doesn't want divorce? " *'I hate divorce,' says the Lord God of Israel, 'and I hate a man's covering himself with violence as well as with his garment,' says the Lord Almighty. So guard yourself in your spirit, and do not break faith* " (Malachi 2:16).

As necessary as divorce is at times, we have to remember that it not only does violence to the marriage relationship itself but also does violence to the family and children from the marriage. God does not hate people who divorce but wants his people, their marriages, and their families to prosper. Just looking forward or looking at a quick solution like divorce won't work in the long run; we must look back for understanding.

Your Heart

In biblical terms, your "heart" is the part of you that feels and that drives much of your actions in everyday life. As Proverbs tells us, *"As water reflects a face, so a man's heart reflects the man"* (27:19). The idea here is that whatever you feel in your heart is at the center of who you are and how you feel about your relationships.

Chances are, you know this already. When you feel loved, honest, and open in relationships, your heart feels at peace and experiences the freedom of being close to another person. If your heart is poisoned with feelings that you are unloved and unappreciated, your heart will hurt and you will feel terrible about yourself. If your relationships are unsafe, threatening, and manipulative, then your heart will shut down as you make efforts to protect yourself.

If your marriage is in trouble, your heart will likely be poisoned with feeling unloved and unsafe. The first step in moving yourself to a better marital relationship is recognizing where your heart hurts and why you do the things you do. Most likely, you and your spouse have hurt each other's hearts by openly criticizing and attacking one another, by being stubborn and defensive with one another, by being hateful, sarcastic, or harsh with one another. Possibly you have shut each other out behind a wall of passivity, hopelessness, or lack of caring for one another. Whatever the interaction (or lack of interaction) with your spouse, it is necessary to get to the core of your feelings.

The following exercise will help you get to the feelings that you have in your heart with regard to being loved and feeling safe in your marital relationship. You do not need to think a lot about every aspect of your relationship with your spouse right now; simply think of the most recent unpleasant episode with your spouse and follow the instructions in the exercise.

EXERCISE 1
Pinpointing Your Emotions

When I am in conflict or argue with my spouse, I generally feel

_____.

(Circle the one, two, or three emotions that best fit the way you feel and then fill in the blank above.)

Unloved	Inadequate	Unsafe	Abandoned
Unworthy	Unacceptable	Insecure	Failure
Insignificant	Hopeless	Disconnected	Rejected
Alone	Unwanted	Unknown	Fearful
Worthless	Not measuring up	Controlled	
Devalued	Powerless	Vulnerable	
Defective	Out of control	Invalidated	

These are your primary emotions with regard to not feeling LOVED and SAFE.

Your History

If your marriage is in trouble, you no doubt identified some heavy and troubling emotions with the exercise above. For almost all of us, however, emotional issues did not begin with our spouses but with how we grew up. This is not to say that your marriage is not the place where you are experiencing the most emotional turmoil; it is simply to say that if you are going to understand what you are doing in your marriage, you need to first begin with your past.

Now, before you might close this book and think, "Oh great, another book that is going to blame all of my problems on my parents," please understand what we are saying. We do not believe that everyone comes from a dysfunctional background and that everyone is "damaged goods" from the beginning. Some of us do come from families that are tough and abusive; some of us come from passive or somewhat manipulative families; and others of us come from pretty good situations. Regardless of your situation, though, it had an effect on you. Think of it this way: If you grew up in a family speaking French, there is an overwhelming chance that you learned to speak French. Likewise, our histories, influenced by the way we were raised, have a large impact on how we view and interact with the world.

You, like all humans, were built to be programmed with important information from your history with those who provided your care. Let's first consider love, because the way you are loved tells you everything you will know about your identity and who you are. If you feel worthy, precious, and valued, you were likely loved in just that way by your parents or caretakers. If you feel unworthy, insignificant, and worthless, you probably picked that program from either bad information or no information from the people who were supposed to love you. You may feel one of these extremes in your heart, or you may simply have nagging feelings that you did not measure up or that you were a disappointment to one of your parents. No matter whether you feel loved, unloved, or something in between, your heart reacts to how it was loved within the family where you grew up.

Let us be clear: You were built to be loved. God loves you in a way that is endless, selfless, and sacrificing. What He said to Israel He would say to each of His children: *"Though the mountains be shaken and the hills be removed, yet my unfailing love for you will not be shaken"* (Isaiah 54:10). Even though your parents or caregivers may not have expressed love to you, God intends you to know that you are precious and worthwhile to Him.

In the same way you were built to be loved, God built you to be programmed in how to trust in relationships. If you came from a family where they provided for your needs, were there for you, were predictable, and taught you how to be responsible, you likely grew up believing that relationships could be safe and secure. If you grew up in a family where the opposite was true, you probably feel wary and suspicious of relationships and are guarded when you interact with others. Of course, some people grew up in families that were between being safe and being damaging. Perhaps you felt overwhelmed with responsibilities that you did not think you could handle or you consistently found yourself being closer to your mother or father than they were to each other. Some families are clearly safe and trustworthy, some are not, and some are between those feeling totally safe and those that damage.

God is resolute in expressing His trustworthiness to us through His faithfulness. He loves us, but He also expects us to trust Him and obey Him. *"Know therefore that the Lord your God is God; he is the faithful God, keeping his covenant to love to a thousand generations of those who love him and keep his commands"* (Deuteronomy 7:9).

So we are built to know who we are by the way we are loved and to be safe by the ways we are taught trustworthiness. Maybe this was done for you growing up and maybe it was not. Perhaps it was done for you partially. For instance, maybe you were loved beyond a shadow of a doubt but your situation was not so safe because you grew up in a family with alcohol or drug abuse. Maybe your family was loving and trustworthy, but your heart was victimized by issues such as racial prejudice or crime. Whatever the source, violations of love and trust make you feel a deep sense of pain.

Now let's relate this back to our subject: marriage. The point is that most likely, not all of the painful emotions you are feeling originated with your spouse. For most of us, in fact, the emotions we feel with our spouses are the very same emotions we have experienced since childhood.

These primary emotions from our histories are similar to "hot buttons," representing sensitive issues that existed for us coming into marriage. When these buttons from the past get pushed in our current situations, we are slammed with the weight of emotion that can be summed up as feeling unloved or unsafe. This weight of emotion comes, not just from our marriage, but also from our earlier history.

Now take a little time in **Exercise 2** to clarify your history a bit so you can understand the background of your feelings.

EXERCISE 2
Recalling Your Growing-Up Years

1. Think of one or two stories about your growing up that impacted you deeply. In these situations, what did you learn about who you are as a person? What did you learn about other people and relationships?

   _____

   _____

   _____

2. Still reflecting on your growing-up years, what were the harmful situations, tragedies, or difficulties that negatively affected your perception of yourself or your view of relationships or other people? What were the healthy situations, people, or occurrences that built into you a positive perception of yourself and relationships?

   _____

   _____

   _____

3. What did you learn about marriage in the family you grew up in? What did you learn about trustworthiness and safety in relationships? How is that similar or dissimilar to your marriage?

   _____

   _____

   _____

Day 1

**IDEA
To Remember:**

*Many of your feelings
and coping behaviors
were with you before
your marriage.*

Your Pain and Your Coping

Johnny, a middle-aged man who came to us for help with his marriage, was in a lot of guilt and shame over his behavior. "I just don't know what happens to me," he said. "I know that anger is absolutely the worst thing that I do to my wife and my family. After I get angry and I see all the damage that it does to my family, I swear that I will never get that angry again. But then something happens—big things like a car wreck or little things like the water hose left out—and it will be like I just lose control. I get angry all over again and do the same type of damage that I hate."

Then he asked the question that so many ask: "Why can't I stop myself?"

There is an answer. And it's not just that Johnny needs more willpower.

To understand, consider that physical pain will put a person's body into such distress that it will mobilize coping defenses. The human nervous system has automatic responses that increase our heart rate, respiration rate, and energy level to either battle what is hurting us (fight response) or get out of the situation to avoid further pain (flight response). The way we are made provides us with a wonderful gift, giving us a method to survive.

Emotional pain can put our body in the same level of distress. When we are not loved the way we want or expect, or when we find ourselves in hurtful relationships, our brain mobilizes the same type of energy to protect us either by fighting or by leaving. It is the brain's way of making sure we survive in the face of threat, whether that threat is physical or emotional. If we can understand the emotional pain we feel, then we will likely be able to understand our reactions to that pain as we try to protect and preserve ourselves.

When we have painful emotions such as those identified in **Exercise 1, page 16** —whether through a memory of our history or an unpleasant interaction with our spouse—our brains are built to react quickly to cope with the pain. Just as with anything that our brain practices, we begin to integrate it as a preferred style or a habit. In Johnny's case, when he feels painful emotions, his brain is practiced to respond with anger. But many of us will have different automatic reactions. For instance, if we feel unloved or unwanted, we might tend to withdraw from relationships. We will probably withdraw every time we run across that emotion in the future. The brain tends to practice what it is used to doing.

It is then almost automatic to start practicing as a habit certain reactions or coping strategies toward particular feelings. Remember, we practice these reactions or habits because we believe they will help us survive our emotional pain. Our reactions are totally understandable given the reality that we are simply trying to cope with painful feelings of not being loved or not feeling safe.

The problem is that these reactions become more automatic to us—even the reactions we hate. For instance, we may hate ourselves for always nagging at our spouse, blowing up in anger, running away into addictive behaviors, or going overboard in trying to control situations. We know that these behaviors only complicate our marriage and relationships, yet when the next situation occurs that causes us stress or pain, we find ourselves again committing the same behavior we hate.

Is this beginning to make sense in the context of your own life? You may begin to grasp the words in Proverbs 26:11: *"As a dog returns to its vomit, so a fool repeats his folly."* You do unproductive coping behaviors over and over again, not because you are weak or stupid, but because your brain has been habituated to cope with painful and distressing feelings in the same way. In other words, when you feel unloved or unsafe, you are into your coping behavior literally before you even realize what you feel.

It is hard to face the reality that you have some reactions to your pain that are not so acceptable or appealing. Right now, however, it is important not to judge yourself but rather to simply get the truth out regarding what you normally do when you feel pain. Knowing the pain you feel and the coping reactions you have is an important step in knowing your heart well enough to get to the bottom of the problems in your marriage.

IDEA
To Remember:

Reactions to pain become more and more automatic to us—even reactions that we hate.

Exercise 3 can help you identify some of your usual reactions to pain.

EXERCISE 3
Pinpointing Your Coping Behaviors

1. When I feel the way I have identified in Exercise 1, page 16, I normally cope through these behaviors:

_____

_____

(Circle the one, two, or three coping behaviors that best fit the way you act.)

Blame others	Negative	Defensive	Numb out
Rage	Anxious	Judging	Impulsive
Angry	Inconsolable	Demanding	View pornography
Sarcastic	Catastrophizing	Critical	Avoid issues
Arrogant	Whiny/needy	Nagging	Hide information
Aggressive	Manipulates	Lecture	Get dramatic
Threatening	Withdraw to pout	Withdraw to defend	Act selfish
Hold grudges	Isolate	Intellectualize	Minimizes
Retaliatory	Fault-finding	Escape	Withdraw to avoid
Withdraw to punish	Perform	Drink	
Shame self	Controlling	Irresponsible	
Depressed	Perfectionistic	Use drugs	

These are the primary coping behaviors you use to deal with lack of LOVE and to try and be SAFE in relationships.

Day 1

Putting Emotions and Coping Together to Understand

If you place the primary emotions that you feel when in conflict with your spouse beside how you find yourself coping or reacting in the relationship, then you will get a pretty good understanding of how you operate when you feel pain. To understand this better, let's consider a couple named Bill and Sandy. We'll be returning to them throughout the book.

Bill's history. Bill comes from a family in which he was the middle of three siblings. Bill's parents were caring people, but his father was somewhat passive. As a result of this passivity, Bill was never quite sure while growing up whether he was pleasing his father. Bill strove to achieve more and more success in order to try and get a more emotional reaction from his father, but his father simply was more distant and did not give much approval or disapproval, praise or criticism.

Bill's mother, on the other hand, was a take-charge type of person. She was the one who usually set the direction in the family and was not slow in making suggestions for what family members needed to do to be successful or correct problems. It was not that she was critical so much as she was involved in every aspect of the family and the leader in setting direction. Bill's father was more than happy to allow her to have this position and went along with almost all of her suggestions. Bill, however, felt smothered by his mother's suggestions and felt she interfered with his life. He learned from an early age to try and keep his relationships, business, and—certainly—his emotions to himself. When his mother would try and find out more, Bill would counter by giving her less. Even though his mother meant well and simply wanted to give him direction, he consistently felt that anything he did would never measure up to his mother's expectations.

Bill carries difficulties from deep-seated primary emotions from his family. He had the sensitivity and worry that he was insignificant and was unacceptable in some regard to his father. He felt that his efforts to make connection were unnoticed and he was unappreciated. Regarding his mother, he felt unsafe and controlled by her and felt that if he became too vulnerable, he would likely not measure up to her standards. In order to cope with this pain, he was often negative about himself and focused on his feelings of self-doubt. But what Bill did most of all was to close off and keep his feelings to himself. He would often isolate himself and be suspicious of any effort that anyone made to get information—a fear that he would be controlled. And Bill withdrew from relationships. He withdrew when his feelings were hurt and he was feeling shameful, and he withdrew to control and protect himself from people knowing or controlling him.

Bill's Feelings

Insignificant
Inadequate
Unaccepted
Unsafe
Controlled
Not measuring up

Bill's Coping

Negative
Withdraws to pout
Invulnerable
Isolates
Closed
Withdraws to defend

Sandy's history. Unlike Bill, Sandy came from a family in which her mother and father were very unhappily married. Sandy's father was a successful business owner who made his only daughter the apple of his eye. He was organized and hard working, and Sandy learned how not to disappoint him, by excelling in school and working to achieve awards that made her daddy proud. Sandy's father, however, was very critical of Sandy's mother, often criticizing her openly for being "incompetent, stupid, and underachieving." Sandy often felt the discomfort of being closer to her father than her mother was and felt disloyal to her mother for not defending her more. Sandy did not have much respect for her mother, because she saw her as weak and dependent upon her father, but she consistently pitied and felt sorry for her mother.

When Sandy was in her early teens, she discovered that her father was having a long-term affair with one of his employees. Despite the airing of this affair, Sandy's parents stayed together, their relationship changing little. Apparently Sandy's mom wasn't concerned much about the affair. Sandy, however, felt that her hero dad had been removed from a pedestal and that he had betrayed her by living a lie. She felt that all the love her father expressed toward her as a youngster was unreliable. She began to doubt herself more and more as she felt that if she could not trust her father, she certainly could not trust what her father said about her.

Sandy felt this pain deeply. As a result, she would often cope by blaming and getting angry about the lies and betrayal. Whenever she saw anything suspicious or unsafe, Sandy would feel those old feelings that reminded her of the past, often responding out of suspicion and anger. In addition, Sandy felt unsafe and abandoned by both her parents. To cope, she would try to depend on herself only and set strict demands on how things should be done and whether they were done acceptably.

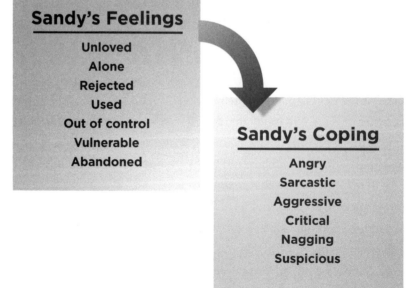

Sandy's Feelings

Unloved
Alone
Rejected
Used
Out of control
Vulnerable
Abandoned

Sandy's Coping

Angry
Sarcastic
Aggressive
Critical
Nagging
Suspicious

Bill and Sandy's Pain Cycle. Both Bill and Sandy have feelings that get activated when they interact, and in the process they both draw on coping strategies in an attempt to feel loved and safe. Here is the real problem: The coping behaviors and strategies that they choose to try and make themselves more lovable and safe are the very strategies that are distancing them further from the things they want in their marriage relationship.

When Bill is not feeling good about himself for a variety of reasons related to his work or interactions, he has that familiar pain of feeling inadequate and insignificant. Instead of seeking to get correct information about himself and connect to Sandy, he copes by isolating, withdrawing, and acting negative and unhappy.

What does this do to Sandy? You guessed it: it smacks her sensitive feelings and issues like a sledgehammer, and she feels vulnerable, alone, and abandoned, just as she did from her parents' relationship. Predictably, Sandy copes with these painful feelings by being critical, angry, and sarcastic with Bill. She presses him and demands that he act in a better way in order to make her feel better.

What does this do to Bill in turn? It slams his issues hard and he feels that Sandy is trying to control him and that she does not love or want him. He withdraws and isolates himself toward the edge of giving up.

But it does not stop there. This behavior simply escalates Sandy's feelings that the situation with Bill is unsafe, insecure, and out of control. In response, she becomes more controlling, angry, and demanding, believing that a solution to her feelings is just around the corner. As she presses in, demands more, and tries to get more out of Bill, he feels more unsafe, unwanted, and inadequate, leading him to be even unhappier, more negative, and more withdrawn. This leads Sandy right back to the place where she feels alone, unloved, unsafe, and used to the point that relating to Bill becomes intolerable.

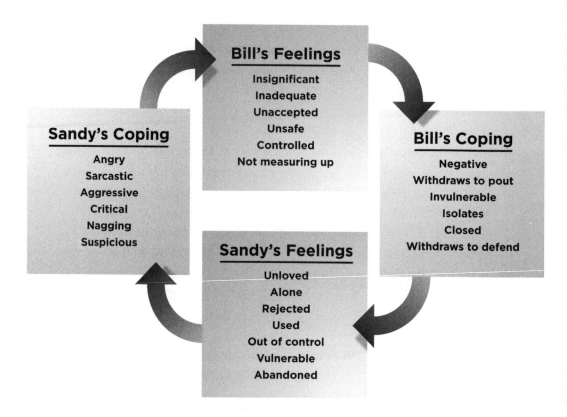

If this process looks like a vicious cycle to you, then you are absolutely on target. Several types of therapy and education, from Emotionally Focused Therapy to Practical Application of Intimate Relationship Skills to the National Institute of Marriage, have identified types of cycles. What we have identified here is called the Pain Cycle, and it represents the process that couples get into that deteriorates their relationships.

If you were to listen in on the conflicts of Bill and Sandy, you would hear them go at one another in seemingly endless ways. Bill would say things like "You just don't understand the way I feel. You are so controlling and demanding. Fine, I will just stop feeling anything, and you are always the one who is right. Just leave me alone, and I will take care of my own business!"

Sandy would say things like, "You are such a wimp. You never are around, and then when you finally tell me something, it is always whining or feeling sorry for yourself. You hide out. You act like there is nothing you can do to improve your situation. Why don't you stop complaining and start doing? I can't take your moodiness anymore!"

You see, Bill and Sandy are attacking each other at the point of their coping behaviors. When the two are in the midst of a fight, Bill really believes that the problems in their marriage are caused by Sandy's judging, angry, controlling, and demanding behavior. Sandy really believes that the problem is Bill's negative, isolating, and withdrawing behavior. In actuality, both Sandy and Bill have feelings of pain that prompt these automatic reactions. Those automatic reactions are actually coping behaviors and are the very things that cause the other more pain.

Couldn't they just change the way they cope? It sounds easy. The problem is that, instead of changing their own behavior, they choose to point the finger at the other. Bill tells Sandy she needs to change her behavior, and Sandy tells Bill what he needs to change. How is this approach working out for them? You know the answer. It is not working, and they have been stuck in this Pain Cycle for years.

The Pain Cycle does not occur once a week or once a month. This is the cycle behind all the other problems in their marriage. They do not have one hundred fights on subjects such as parenting, finances, in-laws, and sex. They have this Pain-Cycle fight one hundred times regardless of the subject.

When trying to discuss their sexual intimacy, for example, Bill feels unwanted, alone, and as though he does not measure up. He copes by withdrawing. This, in turn, leads Sandy to feel used, unsafe, insecure, and out of control. She copes by pressing harder, demanding performance, and trying to get things her way. Immediately, they are back into the full-blown Pain Cycle, damaging one another's feelings of love and safety and deteriorating the relationship. They are not arguing about sex anymore but about the basic level of pain they feel and have been carrying with them since childhood. This Pain Cycle is the root of all arguments in their marriage, regardless of the subject.

You have a cycle in your relationship also. Do not kid yourself into thinking that the problem really is about the money, parenting, sex, or in-laws. These are secondary subjects that can never be solved in your marriage until you get to the root of all these subjects in the Pain Cycle. Take the time to complete the Pain Cycle found in **Exercise 4, page 32**. Be as honest as you can with the issues you identify. It is best if you can fill out your part of the Pain Cycle and have your spouse fill out his or hers. If your spouse is unwilling at this point to do so, simply ask your spouse about some of his or her feelings and coping behaviors when your spouse has those feelings. If your spouse is unwilling to talk with you about it at all, that is okay.

EXERCISE 4
Identifying Your Pain Cycle

1. Complete the Pain Cycle on the next page for you and your spouse.

2. When you look at the Pain Cycle on page 32, think about the most recent disagreements or problems you have had with your spouse. Do you find yourself having some of these feelings and doing some of these coping behaviors when you and your spouse are in conflict?

   _____

3. Think about the last three conflicts you have had with your spouse. In these conflicts, did the Pain Cycle get activated with you? Did you and your spouse start arguing along the path of the Pain Cycle and leave the original issue?

   _____

4. When your spouse does his or her coping behaviors, make special note of how these actions activate your feelings. Notice also that your coping behaviors hit the same sensitive feelings that impact your spouse.

   _____

EXERCISE 4
Identifying Your Pain Cycle

Fill in the Pain Cycle following the instructions.
If your spouse does not want to participate,
just get your cycle down.

Your Feelings

(Write in the emotions
you identified in
Exercise 1, page 16)

1. _____
2. _____
3. _____
4. _____
5. _____

Your Coping

(Write in the coping
behaviors you identified
in Exercise 3, page 23)

1. _____
2. _____
3. _____
4. _____
5. _____

Your Spouse's Coping

(Write in the coping behaviors
your spouse identified
in Exercise 3, page 23)

1. _____
2. _____
3. _____
4. _____
5. _____

Your Spouse's Feelings

(Write in the emotions
your spouse identified in
Exercise 1, page 16)

1. _____
2. _____
3. _____
4. _____
5. _____

> # IDEA
> ## To Remember:
>
> *The ways you protect yourself often hurt your spouse or push him or her away.*

Day 1

Your Responsibility

Because the Pain Cycle is a cycle, it means we can intervene anywhere on this cycle and produce different results in the relationship. In other words, if you work on your own pain and your own reactions, you can have a dynamic effect on the direction of your marriage. You may be tempted to say that your spouse has to do the work first, but the truth is that your spouse is sitting on the other side of the cycle saying the same thing about you. You are the only one who can take responsibility for changing yourself.

It will not be a wasted effort. Most likely, the change you make in yourself will produce the change you are looking for in your marriage. It may not be perfect, but if you keep at the process, it will produce fruit. Even if it does not produce all the change you want in your marriage, it will produce a change in you. You will become more fulfilled as an individual as you grow, and your relationships will become more satisfying.

James says, *"Do not merely listen to the word, and so deceive yourselves. Do what it says"* (1:22). In part, this means that personal issues belong to us individually and are ours to correct. We can always point to the issues that belong to our spouses as an excuse not to deal with ourselves, but that is just the kind of deception that this verse wants us to avoid. Changing ourselves is always the place to begin if we want our life, relationships, and marriage to be different.

Someone else, even someone as close as your mate, is not responsible for your feelings or the coping behaviors you resort to in order to deal with those feelings. In the end, only you can be responsible to make the intervention necessary on these feelings and behaviors. You are not responsible to change your spouse's behavior or feelings and are absolutely not to blame for the way your spouse feels or behaves. Focus on reckoning with and preparing to change your own issues. If you can take responsibility for dealing with your own pain and changing your behavior, which we will show you how to do in Chapter 2, you are on your way to a new marriage.

With that said, there are some situations where you must be careful and guarded with your heart. In situations where your spouse is physically or emotionally abusive, you need to protect yourself before you start trying to change your behavior. We recommend that you seek help from a shelter or a counselor in order to provide interventions to protect yourself and, possibly, your children.

We also believe it is necessary to first get some outside help through counseling in those cases where your spouse is having an active affair or is carrying on an active addiction. In these situations, if the pursuit of another person or substance has become the most important thing in a spouse's life, it is highly unlikely that anything you do will produce change in the relationship. Hope that these situations can be turned around may exist, but a skilled counselor needs to address them before you take on the responsibility to change only yourself.

In short, active abuse, affairs, and addictions need help beyond what this book addresses.

Beyond these exceptions, however, we encourage you to take a long and hard look at your part of the cycle and not concentrate on how your spouse needs to change. Slow down your automatic coping and reacting by making sure you are in touch with your own feelings. Get in touch with how these primary emotions of pain in your life have been present for many years, and take the time to know them well. Recognize your part in making the Pain Cycle destructive to your marriage.

To quote James again, *"Everyone should be quick to listen, slow to speak and slow to become angry"* (1:19). If you can just look at your own pain, understand that you have been a part of a cycle, and realize that you must take responsibility for your own part of the cycle, then you have done the necessary work for the first day.

For Reflection

1. Allow yourself to remember some of the painful interactions and relationships from your family growing up and from your marriage. Say a short prayer for God's help in dealing effectively with pain.

2. Consider the Pain Cycle that you and your spouse have been engaged in from **Exercise 4, page 31**. Ask God's help in giving you the strength and insight to deal with changing these old coping behaviors.

3. Meditate on the following verses: *"He chose us in him before the creation of the world to be holy and blameless in his sight. In love he predestined us to be adopted as his sons through Jesus Christ, in accordance with his pleasure and will—to the praise of his glorious grace, which he has freely given us in the One he loves"* (Ephesians 1:4-6).

4. From the *5 Days to a New Marriage* App: **Day 1**, complete the Pain Cycle exercise to identify pain from the past and the coping behaviors associated with the descriptors. *Download the 5 Days to a New Marriage app from your App Store, search "New Marriage."*

The Peace Cycle
Reestablishing the Truth to Get Healthy

Day 2

"Now that I know what is wrong, what do I do about it?"

If you found yourself asking this question at the end of the previous chapter, then you are right where most of us are when we finally see the problem in our marriage. It's great to understand our Pain Cycle—it explains a lot. But that understanding is just the beginning. Nothing has changed yet.

If you were to stop at this point, it would be like going to the doctor with a severe ailment, getting a thorough examination, sitting patiently on that table with the butcher paper covering it, listening to the doctor give you a clear diagnosis of what is wrong with your body—and then watching him walk out of the room. You would yell through the door, "Thanks for telling me what is wrong, but what do I do now?"

As essential as it is to know where we get off track and go in wrong directions with our feelings and actions in our marriages, it does no good if we don't have a clear map of where to go to find the right direction. So Day 2 in the *Five Days to a New Marriage* approach is about capitalizing on the truth that you can make changes in yourself that will ultimately change your marital system. You see, you have more power than you think. You are not simply stuck, helplessly and hopelessly waiting for your spouse to make changes so that you can feel okay. Now that you know something about your Pain Cycle, it is time to make some changes.

Surely you don't enjoy some of the behaviors you exhibit when you are feeling unloved and unsafe. Aren't you tired of feeling that way? There is a better way, one that is healthier for you and more beneficial for your marriage. You can convert your Pain Cycle into a Peace Cycle. You can change your emotions from negative to positive through believing truths instead of lies, and thus you can change your reactions from unhelpful automatic reactions to helpful deliberate choices. And then, as your behaviors change, your spouse's reactions to you will change too—and you'll be on your way to a new marriage.

IDEA
To Remember:

You have more power to change your marriage than you think.

The Truth about You

God designed you to experience unconditional love and acceptance. You were supposed to grow up in a totally safe and secure home. God's desire was for your childhood to be a continuous reinforcement of His love for you and your ability to trust in Him. He wanted that for your closest relationships on earth as well—for you to experience love and be surrounded by people who were trustworthy.

As we identified in Chapter 1, however, not many of us had this kind of experience. Instead, we experienced losses, hurts, disappointments, and pain. Those who meant the most to us consistently or eventually let us down. We know where that path leads.

Listen to Lisa and how desperate her heart wants to believe something different about herself. "I just don't know if there is anything inside of me that is worthy or worthwhile," she says. "Seriously, I look at who I am and what I do and I can't imagine anything good about myself or why anyone would ever want to have anything to do with me. I feel flawed and rejected. Sometimes I think that it is no wonder that I have so many strange coping behaviors, because I feel so strange on the inside."

You may feel like Lisa and assume that you already know the truth about yourself—and it's not pretty. But God's desires for you are very different. That's because loving interactions allow people to feel worthy, valuable, and significant. And because safe environments lead people to feel secure and capable. In fact, God's design looks like the opposite of your old feelings in the Pain Cycle.

While your spouse and your marital situation are at work pushing your buttons, God is behind the scenes waiting to remind you of the truth. You are not unwanted; God longs for relationship with you. You are not insignificant; the Creator of the universe valued you so much that He sent His only Son to die for you. You are not defective; God knit you together in your mother's womb, and He makes no junk. You are not abandoned or alone; He will never leave you or forsake you.

God's truth is the opposite of the feelings of pain you carry around, and He longs for you to understand the truth about yourself. As Jesus said, *"You will know the truth, and the truth will set you free"* (John 8:32). Aren't you tired of lugging these painful emotional buttons around for people (especially your spouse) to push? Don't you get tired of feeling unloved and unsafe in key relationships in your life? Of course you do; we all do. And that is the beauty of God's system. The truth frees us from the power of these old painful feelings.

Furthermore, God has a truth that is specifically designed for each of us to counter these emotions. Complete **Exercise 5, page 40**, to determine the truths that are opposite the feelings that are part of your old Pain Cycle.

EXERCISE 5
Learning the Truth about Yourself

1. Go back to the previous exercise (page 31) and write down words that describe your emotions when you feel pain.

   My emotions when I feel pain are _____.

   Take a look at the list below. These words are descriptive of the truth about who you are and how God looks at you.

2. The truth about me and my situation is that I am _____.
   (Circle the words that seem to be the opposite of the words that you chose before or words that are significant to you.)

The Truth about You

Loved	Valued	Wanted	Adequate
Priceless	Accepted	Can make choices	Celebrated
Treasured	Promising	Valuable	Encouraged
Appreciated	Significant	Known	Connected
Full of worth	Precious	Never alone	Can control self

The Truth about Your Safety with God

Persisting through trials	Sure that all will work for good
Forgiven and restored	Powerful to protect self
Free to be different	Connected to God and His people
Never forsaken	Validated that your efforts count
Secure that God is just	God will provide for you
Able to affect situation	In control of self
Protected from the victory of evil	Known by God and able to be open
Successful and able to persist	Measuring up in God's grace

Making the Truth Real

Exercise 5 probably just seems like you are putting words on a page. That's okay. In reality, you have at least three ways to tap into the power of these self-truths.

The three critical sources of truth are these: God's truth, trusted people in your life, and yourself.

First source of truth: God. Of the three sources, God's truth is the most powerful because God knows the most about you—not the "you" that is a product of your upbringing, but the "you" that He designed. And this truth comes through two different but completely compatible channels: the Holy Spirit and the Holy Scriptures.

It was no accident that Jesus described the Holy Spirit as the "Spirit of truth." You hear from God through the Holy Spirit by praying and listening. This may test your theology a little, but God really wants to speak to you. Specifically, He wants you to know the truth about yourself. He does not want His children running around down here feeling unloved and unsafe. So the Holy Spirit reminds us of the truth.

Try it out. Find a quiet place and read your list of feelings in the Pain Cycle to God. For each feeling, ask Him if this is true about you. Are you really unworthy, invaluable, and abandoned (or whatever feelings you have)? Wait for His response. It may take a while, or even a few tries, if you are not used to hearing God.

We worked with one guy who so desperately wanted to hear the truth from God that he went away to pray at every break in our meetings. Finally, on the third morning, he came to breakfast excited to tell everyone that the Holy Spirit had spoken to him in the shower and told him that he was indeed valuable. Later that morning, he and his wife got into an argument, and all the old painful feelings got activated in his cycle. The man disappeared for a little while and finally showed up at lunch with a wet head. He told the group that he had gone back to the shower so that God could remind him of the truth of his value. By the end of the week, the entire group was clamoring to get into the "shower where God spoke."

Fortunately, you don't need a shower. God can use the Holy Spirit to remind you of the truth anywhere. You just have to slow down and ask for God to speak to you.

God will also use the Bible as a channel to share His truth with you. It might be worth taking each of your feelings in the Pain Cycle and finding a verse from Scripture that lines up directly against it. For example, someone with a fear of being abandoned might want to memorize Hebrews 13:5, which says, *"Never will I leave you; never will I forsake you."* The Bible is the written truth of God, and some of us just need to see things in black and white.

We are told many times in the Bible to take the Word of God and *"inscribe it on the tablet of our heart"* or to *"hide it in our heart."* Why would God have us do that? Because He knows that we have these old and painful feelings in our heart from past experiences, and if left unchecked, these feelings will cause us to cope in ways to protect ourselves. Instead, God wants His truth inscribed and hidden in our heart so that the old feelings of pain will lose their power. We will know the truth, and we will be free.

Ramond's parents left him to be raised by grandparents. Thinking back to those early years, Ramond said, "I always felt there was something wrong with me, because deep down I didn't think my parents wanted me. But I came across this verse that I think was meant for me: *'For he chose us in him before the creation of the world to be holy and blameless in his sight.'* I may not feel holy and blameless sometimes, but this verse always helps me to center on the fact that I am wanted, I am chosen." Ramon was transformed by the truth in God's Word.

Second source of truth: Trustworthy others. After God's truth through the Holy Spirit and the Bible, the next source of truth for you is trusted people in your life. They can remind you of the realities that, in God, you are valuable, wanted, connected, and so on.

But this source of truth is second on the list for a reason: although good friends can tell you the truth, they can also lead you astray. You must carefully evaluate what people say to you and how they treat you. Healthy friends can easily remind you of the truth about yourself—and this can be very helpful. But catch such people on a bad day, and they may say things to hurt you or behave in ways that hit those feelings in your Pain Cycle hard.

Professional counselors are often more unbiased and objective than your friends, so they can be a better resource to remind you of the truth. But they, too, are less than infallible.

In short, friends and counselors can be good sources of truth because we all need God with skin on every now and then, but they should never completely replace the ultimate source of truth: God Himself. But there's still another source of truth to consider.

Third source of truth: Yourself. We can sit prayerfully and hear the Holy Spirit confirm a word of truth to us, read it in the Scripture, or even hear it from the mouths of our closest and most trusted friends. But if we decide that we are going to reject those truths about ourselves outright—sort of like not allowing a ball to go past the net in tennis—we will bounce the truth right out of our minds and hearts.

IDEA
To Remember:

The critical sources of the truth about you and your situation are God's truth, trusted people in your life, and yourself.

We will, in fact, lie to ourselves and proclaim that those things that God or others say about us are unbelievable. Perhaps we will say something like, "If those folks really knew who I was, they would know that I am not any of those things."

Whatever the reason you reject the truth about yourself or your situation, you are powerful enough to not let it go into your heart. The third source of this truth then, must be yourself!

IDEA To Remember:

Either you will take on these truths and let them into your heart or you will reject them and stay stuck in the same old pain.

This is a great decision time in your life. Either you will take on these truths and let them into your heart or you will reject them and stay stuck in the same old pain. You may protest here and say, "Someone believable needs to show me that I am loved and that I can make it in my situation." We can tell you that you are the only one who can make it believable for yourself.

Bob always wanted this reassurance. He told us, "I keep saying that someone owes me the words I want to hear. I want them to say I'm a precious and valuable person. I want them to say I'm worthwhile. But when someone says it, it has no effect on me. I automatically reject it. Worse yet, I reject it when I read verses that tell me that I'm loved. Despite what I say, I really want people to say things to me that I myself refuse to believe. I have to be willing to believe it myself or what others or even God says about me just won't go in!"

Bob is starting to get it. How about you?

Think about it as if you were raising children. Almost everyone who is sane would want to teach children that they are deeply loved, that they are not alone, and that everything possible will be done to make sure they are protected and safe. This is what parents do for their children every day, and it represents the best of who we are. Even though you might have come from a situation or family where it was not done for you to the point where you felt loved or felt safe, you do possess the desire to make it happen for children dependent upon you.

It is helpful to realize that you are now that adult for yourself. You have these needs to repair the damaged self and allow yourself to be loved. You require a safe and secure environment that is protected. You would do this for a child, and now it is time to do it for yourself. In other words, it is time for you to re-parent yourself! It is time for you to care for yourself enough to allow the messages of care and nurture from the Holy Spirit, the Bible, and the trusted people in your life into your heart.

No one is powerful enough to make you accept the truth about yourself except you. Will you accept that truth?

Moving the Truth into Action

So what does all this truth stuff have to do with healing your marriage? Good question. As you identified in Chapter 1, when old feelings in the Pain Cycle get activated, you cope to protect yourself, thus activating the painful feelings of your spouse … and so the Pain Cycle rages on. To break the cycle, something has to change.

Remember Bill and Sandy from Chapter 1? When Bill gets his pain hit and feels unaccepted, inadequate, and controlled, his old coping style kicks in and he becomes negative, withdrawn, and closed off. When Sandy feels unloved, alone, and vulnerable, she fires up the coping fuel of anger, criticism, and nagging. In order to break the old Pain Cycle, they both have to remember the truths about themselves. The truth about Bill is that he is absolutely acceptable, perfectly adequate, and in control of himself. Sandy is not unloved, alone, and vulnerable but instead is deeply loved, never alone, and secure that God is in control.

We do have to warn you about something: this is easy to do on a piece of paper and much harder to do when your spouse is actually pushing your buttons. You can fill out the chart in **Exercise 5, page 40**, in the privacy of your room, but it is much harder to remind yourself of the truth when your spouse is rejecting you or trying to control you. That is when it is most critical to call a timeout or find a place to remind yourself of the truth.

Take a moment to meditate on the truths you listed in **Exercise 5, page 40**. It is probably a pretty powerful set of words. You long to hear these words from your spouse, your God, and the most important people in your life. You are valuable; you are worthy; you are not alone; you are safe—whatever you listed. These could be called *"desires of your heart,"* and God longs to give you the desires of your heart (Psalm 37:4). God wants you to feel these things. He wants your spouse to reinforce them in your life too. But even if your spouse does not cooperate, God wants you to be constantly aware of the truth and decide that you will accept it as truth in your life. You must be willing to hear these things from yourself even

> # IDEA
> ## To Remember:
>
> *Personal truths free you to respond with actions and behaviors that are naturally healthy for your marriage.*

if you do not hear them from others. God wants you to hear it from Him and He wants you to hear it from yourself.

Moving Away from the Old Coping

Remembering the truth is the first step to breaking the Pain Cycle. The second step is just as important because it targets the other portion of your Pain Cycle—those coping strategies you use to protect yourself (becoming angry, manipulating, withdrawing, criticizing, or whatever they may be). These behaviors are the things that really hurt your spouse.

We are not proud of these behaviors. You don't hear people saying, "Man, I am really proud of how I withheld love and affection from my spouse," or "I really said some positive things during that raging outburst yesterday." These coping behaviors are not consistent with how we were designed. God did not intend us to build walls and disconnect from important people in our life, nor did He knit us together to protect ourselves at all costs with angry, threatening, aggressive behaviors.

You were designed to be open, connected, loving, and accepting. Read that list again. Can you believe that? Open, connected, loving, and accepting—are those words your spouse would use to describe you? Are those words you would use to describe the coping strategies that you identified for yourself in **Exercise 3, page 22**? Probably not.

But what if the cycle changed? What if instead of feeling unloved and unsafe with your old Pain Cycle, you rested in the truth about yourself?

We have found that people who are able to replace the old painful feelings with the truth are then able to replace coping strategies with healthier ways of relating. They behave in more positive ways. They are free to respond and act in ways that are consistent with how God designed them. They show empathy and compassion for their spouse; they communicate, slow down, and listen; they apply truth in ways that change the interactions with their spouse for the better. In short, they replace coping strategies with action-oriented loving responses.

Hal had trouble getting to the truth, but when he did, it made all the difference in the world. Here is what he said when talking to his wife: "I find myself so locked into feeling unloved and unwanted that the only thing that I want to do is to strike back at you. I want to make you feel rejected! I want you to feel as badly as I do! (Pause.) But the truth ... the truth ... the truth is that I know myself that I belong and that you are not responsible for making me feel okay. I have to be okay with myself. (Heaves a heavy sigh.) When I'm okay with myself, I don't want to hurt you but I want to love you. I do love you."

When you are walking in the truth, your actions line up with the good things God says should naturally flow from His children, things like *"love, joy, peace, patience, kindness, goodness, faithfulness, gentleness and self-control"* (Galatians 5:22-23). The idea here is clear: When you tie into the truth about yourself concerning how you are loved by God and how God is trustworthy, you will find yourself responding with the natural actions that lead to healthy interactions.

You have been created with the ability to connect in loving ways to the people around you. These connections are fortified by actions and behaviors that communicate care and facilitate healthy connection. In **Exercise 6, page 49**, take the time to identify the ways you want to respond when you are operating in your truth. These actions are likely to be the opposite of how you used to react when your pain feelings got hit in the old cycle.

What the New Behavior Looks Like

It is incredibly important that you identify the ways you want to respond and act when you are interacting with your spouse. As you get more comfortable with the truth about who you are, these actions will flow more and more easily. Some will flow more naturally because they are in line with the way God knit you together and gifted you (for example, an empathetic person will naturally care and show compassion). Even if they don't seem to come easily, we all have the capacity to act in ways that will bless our spouse and improve our marriages. Identify the actions you want to utilize in your marriage and start applying them.

Day 2

EXERCISE 6
Choosing Your New Actions

1. When I have identified the truth in Exercise 5, page 40, I can find strength to act in the following ways:

_____

_____

(Circle the one, two, three, or four ways that you feel you can act if you are living in your truth.)

Accepting	Nondefensive	Energetic
Nurturing	Vulnerable	Hopeful
Supportive	Communicate care	Respectful
Encouraging	Engaging	Open
Giving	Peaceful	Intimate
Welcoming	Let go/relax	Able to persist
Kind	Settled	Responsible
Gentle	Seeking good	Trustworthy
Listening	Merciful	Honest
Empathetic	Loving	Reliable
Humble	Valuing self	Stay connected
Inclusive	Positive	Self-controlled
Patient	Joyful	Transparent
Forgiving	Show compassion	Turn from addictive behaviors

Let's think about Bill from Chapter 1. When he is in tune with how God loves him and how God is trustworthy, he is able to accept the truth that he is significant, accepted, secure, and powerful. In this truth, he is able to remember and choose to act in ways that change his marriage for the better: Bill is able to be a positive encourager and stay connected to intimate relationships.

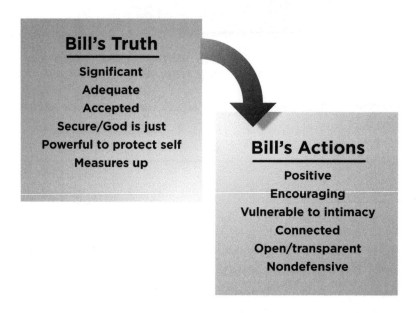

Now let's think about Sandy, Bill's wife. When Sandy gets down to the truth of who she is in God and her situation in God, she finds that she is not unloved and alone but instead deeply and passionately loved in such a way that she will not be rejected or ever alone. Instead of being vulnerable and abandoned the way that she was in her family, she can rest in the truth that God is with her, that He is just and will work things for eventual good, and that she can persist by faith and not just be dependent on herself.

When she ties into these truths about who she is and her relationship to God, she is able to make some significantly different choices on how to behave in her marriage. Sandy is free to be nurturing and supportive. She is not dependent on controlling, nagging, and being suspicious but instead can act much more balanced and fair in relationships, not insisting on her own way and accepting of imperfection.

Sandy's Truth

Loved
Never alone
Valued
Secure that God is just
In control of self
Powerful to protect self
Never forsaken

Sandy's Actions

Nurturing
Supportive
Respectful
Balanced/fair
Accepting of imperfections
Not insistent on own way

The Peace Cycle

This process of understood truth leading to healthy behaviors is consistent and amazingly powerful. The Bible tells us that at the time of Jesus' baptism God declared to Him, *"You are my Son, whom I love; with you I am well pleased"* (Mark 1:11). In so doing, God reminded Him of the truth. And what did Jesus do next? Following this affirmation by His Father, He went on to minister to others through actions that changed their lives: teaching, healing, serving, leading, and showing compassion.

Can you believe that? This is a process God used on His own Son. You have to believe He wants to see this same process utilized in your life.

Are you ready to take advantage of this powerful process? Are you ready to operate in the truth with a clear understanding of the actions that will flow from there?

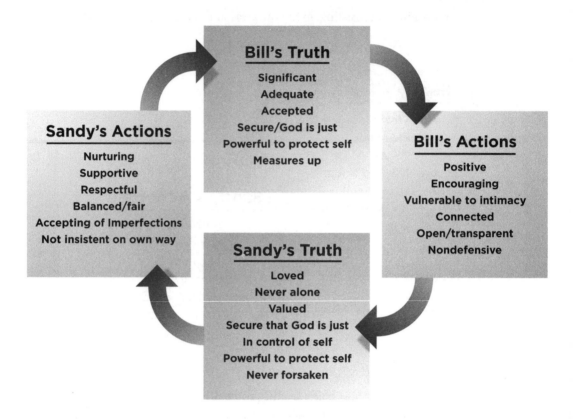

If so, you are ready to move out of the Pain Cycle that you identified in Chapter 1. Your relationships no longer need to be characterized by hurt, anger, and disconnection. You deserve better. You need some peace.

It is easy to see that if Bill and Sandy are operating out of their truths and acting in ways that build their marriage, then their relationship works much better. As Bill is more positive, encouraging, connected, and open with Sandy, she feels loved, valued, not alone, and safe. As Sandy has these feelings of being loved and safe, she in turn is more nurturing, accepting, and respectful in balancing her control with what Bill wants and needs. As she acts in these loving ways, Bill will feel adequate, accepted, and like he measures up.

You see, as Bill and Sandy stay grounded in their own truths, they are more and more likely to behave in ways that are loving, which confirm the truths in each other. When they do this, they do more than just get along better. They experience harmony and a healthy spot in their marriage. It is more than just feeling good. It is feeling at peace.

If that cycle looks a little too good to be true, you are almost right. It takes a lot of work to pull this off, but it is possible and it is worth it. It is called the Peace Cycle because couples operating together in their truth, and acting in ways that connect them, experience positive interactions that once seemed incomprehensible. This is what marriage was designed to look like—couples working together to achieve unity, love, trust, and safety. In other words, peace.

You can have this cycle in your relationship. Start with what you can control. Your half of the equation is your truth and your actions. Fill in the Peace Cycle in **Exercise 7, page 54**. Use your responses from **Exercise 5, page 40**, (your truths) and **Exercise 6, page 49**, (your actions). As was the case in your Pain Cycle, see if you can get your spouse to fill in that part.

Again, these may feel like nothing more than words you have written on a page in a book. But in reality, you have so much more. You have a greater understanding of how you were knit together, what the truth is about you, and how you can act differently in your relationship. This awareness is critical to changing your life. God wants to see you operating in this manner. That means that, whether or not your spouse is willing to cooperate at this point, you have the greatest teammate in the world—God Himself—on your side. And that changes everything.

Imagine for a moment how your life will be different if you choose to actively engage the behaviors you listed in **Exercise 6, page 49**. What kind of things would you do? What would your interactions with important people in your life look like? How would you treat your spouse differently?

EXERCISE 7
Creating Your Peace Cycle

Fill in the Peace Cycle following the instructions.
If your spouse does not want to participate,
just get your cycle down.

Your Truths

(Write in the truths
you identified in
Exercise 5, page 40)

1. _____
2. _____
3. _____
4. _____
5. _____

Spouse's Actions

(Write in the new actions
your spouse identified in
Exercise 6, page 49)

1. _____
2. _____
3. _____
4. _____
5. _____

Your Actions

(Write in the new actions
you identified in
Exercise 6, page 49)

1. _____
2. _____
3. _____
4. _____
5. _____

Spouse's Truths

(Write in the truths
your spouse identified in
Exercise 5, page 40)

1. _____
2. _____
3. _____
4. _____
5. _____

What if you try a little experiment? Start your day tomorrow with some time with God. Ask Him to remind you of the truths you identified in **Exercise 5, page 40**. Then review the actions list from **Exercise 6, page 49**. Commit to operating in and utilizing these behaviors in your relationships and interactions throughout the day. You don't have anything to lose, so give it a try!

A Little Extra You Can Do by Yourself

You can now see how both spouses can work together to create a healthy marital environment characterized by peace. But whether your spouse is willing to participate or not, you have a great deal of power to live as the person you were designed by God to be. Living from your truth and responding with healthy actions will make a difference in your marriage.

And there is one more thing you can do by yourself to improve your chances of success. Observation of thousands of marriages makes it clear that there is something that individuals in the best marriages have. This "something" is not usually present in poor marriages. As a matter of fact, the happiest people in the world (married or single) understand this "something." The "something" is a person's ability to care for himself or herself enough to stay whole, full, and healthy.

You see, we are a culture loaded down with empty, exhausted people. We are a hurried, frantic people who are rushing from one place to the next. All of the chaos leaves us tired and worn out. From this empty place, it is difficult to remember the truth about ourselves and the healthy actions we want to exhibit in our marriages. Instead, our hot buttons are exposed, and we get by in survival mode by running on fumes.

So there is a critical secret that you must understand to succeed in your marriage—you need to take care of yourself so that you stay whole, full, and healthy.

Once again, we can turn to Jesus as an example. All we know about Jesus' life as He prepared for the ministry that would change the world is that He grew in four areas: *"Jesus grew in wisdom and stature, and in favor with God and men"* (Luke 2:52). Throughout His ministry, we find examples of Jesus revisiting these four areas to recharge. He knew that He needed to be healthy in these four areas in order to use His gifts and reenergize His strengths for the demanding relationships and tasks He faced. Let's take a closer look at the four areas and what is included in each:

1. **Mentally** (wisdom, mind)—feeding your mind positive messages and images, reading, learning, meditating, having stimulating conversations, focusing your mind on whatever is true and pure

2. **Physically** (stature, strength)—eating healthy, exercising daily, sleeping at least eight hours per day, drinking plenty of water, being adventurous, staying aware of your energy levels

3. **Spiritually** (favor with God, soul)—praying, listening to God, reading the Bible, fellowship with other believers, worshiping through song

4. **Emotionally** (favor with men, heart)—paying attention to your feelings, having healthy friendships, guarding your heart, healthy expression of emotions, fully engaging yourself in activities

Complete **Exercise 8, page 58**, below to see how you are doing in these areas. This exercise is important because there is a basic principle at work here: You can give away only what you have. If your total score in Exercise 8 is a 45, then that is all the energy you have to get you through today, with all the demands on your time, your schedule, and your relationships. If you are a mom with small kids, you can bet that at least the first fifty points on your total score go into taking care of the kids each day. The same is true for a person working outside the home; the first fifty points or so go into our jobs.

If your score is low, is there any wonder that you don't often have loving, deep, meaningful interactions with your spouse at the end of a long day? Neither one of you has anything left to give each other. Instead of having strengths ready to bless each other, you are exhausted with pain feelings near the surface ready to get triggered by the slightest inappropriate facial expression from your spouse.

The solution is simple to read and hard to put into practice but worth the investment. You must take time to get your score up in each of the four areas. Don't just focus on one—each area is critical. The good news is that you can sometimes find one activity that recharges you in more than one area. For example, going for a walk in the woods might fill you physically because of the activity, recharge you mentally because you can relax your mind by unplugging from your cell phone, and reconnect you spiritually as you pray and experience God's creation. Or singing worship songs may recharge you emotionally and spiritually. The goal is to get your score up in each area so that you feel rejuvenated and filled with something you can share with others.

Day

2

IDEA
To Remember:

Healthy people consistently recharge themselves emotionally, spiritually, mentally, and physically.

EXERCISE 8
Rating Your Health

Rate how whole, full, and healthy you feel in each area. Read each summary above and rate where you would fall on the continuum (put the number from 1 to 25 in the blank beside each area).

[---]
   0   5   10   15   20   25

_____ 1. Mentally   _____ 2. Physically   _____ 3. Spiritually   _____ 4. Emotionally

Get a total score by adding your responses in each area. If we think of 100 as the perfect score (being completely whole, full, and healthy in each area), what does your total score say about how healthy you are?

List something you can do in each of the four areas to raise your score.

Mentally, I will _____ .

Physically, I will _____ .

Spiritually, I will _____ .

Emotionally, I will _____ .

For Reflection

1. Meditate on your truths and strengths. How will your interactions with your spouse be different as you live in these truths and utilize your strengths?

2. What would your marriage look like if you consistently scored above 80 on the whole, full, and healthy index? What do you need to start doing to make this happen?

3. From the *5 Days to a New Marriage* App: **Day 2**, create your individual Peace Cycle by completing the exercise to identify truth and healthy, life-giving cycles . *Download the 5 Days to a New Marriage app from your App Store, search "New Marriage."*

"Us-ness"

Reconnecting to the New Self and the New Relationship

Day 3

Seemingly dazed, Jody and Yolanda sat together on the couch during one of our marriage intensives.

Jody spoke up first. "This all sounds great when you put it on paper. We look at that old Pain Cycle stuff and absolutely know it is right and know it is where we have been. We look at the Peace Cycle and really think that would be nice. But the question in our mind is how we are going to move from that place of pain to that place of peace."

Yolanda made the same point in starker terms. "You know what hell is like, but it seems unbelievable to us that we could actually get to heaven. How are we going to get from here to there?"

Getting from "here to there" is what Day 3 is all about. In this chapter we are going to teach you a simple and profound process of moving yourself and your marriage from the Pain Cycle to the Peace Cycle.

You already know how to recognize the old feelings and coping behaviors that make up your Pain Cycle. And you know about the possibility of doing things differently when you stay in your truth and act in the Peace Cycle. But we know how hard it is in the heat of battle to stay out of your old destructive pattern. So we want to say this to you: we have a plan that will help you. It's a well-tested plan that has already helped hundreds of couples with marital problems as bad or worse than your own. You can trust it because it is rooted in a spiritual principle, has good brain science behind it, and is based on good old-fashioned practice.

You may be looking at getting from "here to there" as daunting. But be encouraged, because you can make the process of change work in your marriage. And it will be the means of building up something beautiful, something that in this chapter we will be introducing as "us-ness." But first let's consider the possibility and the means of change.

The New Self

The biggest reason we know that you can make a different choice when it comes to the old Pain Cycle is because we see it in Scripture. *"If anyone is in Christ,"* the apostle Paul says, *"he is a new creation; the old has gone, the new has come!"* (2 Corinthians 5:17). This means that when we come into a relationship with Christ, we are forgiven of our past failures and have a chance to actually be pleasing to God. Our motivations and potential all start to be engaged, and we start to be able to value the things that God values most. God's Holy Spirit is alive and at work in us, moving us toward the things that are best and of God.

But God does not stop there by just making us new in our motivations and desires. His Holy Spirit is also at work in us to make the changes in our nature come to pass. Consider 2 Corinthians 3:18: *"We, who with unveiled faces all reflect the Lord's glory, are being transformed into his likeness with ever-increasing glory, which comes from the Lord, who is the Spirit."* This verse is a way of saying that once we belong to Christ as a new creation, then God through the Holy Spirit continues to work on us to make us more and more like Christ. Imagine that all your values, actions, motivations, desires, and emotions can eventually be absolutely in tune with Jesus. This is the promise. If you belong to Christ, you have already changed. But mainly, if you belong to Christ, you are being changed into His perfect image by the Holy Spirit.

So you may say, "If God has made me a new creation and the Holy Spirit is going to change me, why do I need to do anything?" This is a great question. Throughout the Scriptures we see a picture of how God loves to work with us in partnership. Could He do it by Himself? Well, if God is all powerful, not only could He bring all of creation into existence, but He could also make it run just the way He wanted. But the point is that God created the world in such a way that He was involved in making it run the way He wanted through a partnership with us. He wants us to work together to bring about righteousness, justice, and peace.

God evidently finds great joy in free-willed creatures deciding that they love Him enough to partner with Him. People who love Him enough to remember who He is, who depend on Him enough, who seek the way He does things and cast off their own ways of trying to make things work out—these are the kinds of people whom God wants as partners.

But He does not just want this partnership with us in terms of some job or activity; he wants a partnership based on how He reforms our internal selves. He wants to remake us from the inside out. He could do that all by Himself, but He chooses to partner with us, and He expects us to join in the work of changing ourselves.

The apostle Paul put it memorably: *"You were taught, with regard to your former way of life, to put off your old self, which is being corrupted by its deceitful desires; to be made new in the attitude of your minds; and to put on the new self, created to be like God in true righteousness and holiness"* (Ephesians 4:22-24). In other words, God wants us to work with Him to take off the old self (which is full of all that pain and problem-coping behavior we discussed in Chapter 1) and put on the new self (which is connected to the truth and strengths we talked about in Chapter 2).

Again, listen to how much God wants us to participate in this work of moving from the pain and all the problems it brings to a new sense of self. *"You used to walk in these ways, in the life you once lived. But now you must rid yourselves of all such things as these: anger, rage, malice, slander, and filthy language from your lips. Do not lie to each other, since you have taken off your old self with its practices and have put on the new self, which is being renewed in the knowledge in the image of its Creator"* (Colossians 3:7-10). God is for us and wants our participation in overcoming the pain and behavior of the past. He loves us and deeply desires for us to connect to His truth about who we are and the strengths and gifts He wants us to display. He wants us as partners in taking off our old selves and putting on the new!

IDEA To Remember:

God wants you as a partner in changing your "old self" into your "new self."

Enabling Your Brain to Change

Admittedly, this stuff is hard. Really hard. We can say, "Yes, I am willing to partner with God to put on this new self," but not have any idea how to put it into practice. This is especially true when we are faced with our buttons being pushed by our spouse! How do we make change happen in the midst of an argument? How do we actually do this work?

One of the things that amazes us about Scripture is the fact that it proves more and more to be accurate. The apostle Paul, two thousand years before we understood anything about neuroscience, gave us the answer on how to go about this process of putting on the "new self" and actually changing. *"Do not conform any longer to the pattern of this world,"* he said, *"but be transformed by the renewing of your mind"* (Romans 12:2). Here is the secret to putting on the "new self." We have to be able to renew our mind.

Your brain is made up of billions of connections between nerve cells that "communicate" with one another by firing a message from one cell to another. Long chains of nerve cells are responsible for all our mental activities, the emotions we feel, our recognition of things we have learned, and habits and behaviors we have formed. The field of neuroscience, which is responsible for studying the brain, has made great strides over the past two decades in understanding how it works. What scientists have come to realize is astounding—and particularly applicable to us at two points.

Using existing brain pathways. The first important thing we learn from neuroscience is that the chains of firing neurons that produce thoughts, emotions, and behaviors are used over and over again. In fact, the more we use certain thoughts, emotions, and behaviors, the more we are likely to use those same thoughts, emotions, and behaviors again. In other words, the brain prefers to do what it already knows. Unless there is specific and thoughtful effort to make a change in the way we think, we will most likely reason, feel, and behave the way we are used to doing it in the past.

Think of it like a snow-capped mountain. When the snow melts, where will the water go? The water will find the well-worn low spots, gullies, crevasses, and canyons. It will not create new pathways but instead will go down the pathway of least resistance, thereby making that pathway even more worn.

Your brain works in much the same way. If you don't deliberately intervene, you will think, feel, and act the way you most often do. To put it in real terms, if you normally feel controlled or put down when your spouse gives you a word of correction, the next time your spouse makes a suggestion, you will find yourself feeling controlled or put down. If your normal reaction to this is to fly off the handle in an angry rage, accusing him or her of not being sensitive enough or caring enough, then you will likely find yourself doing the same thing next time. Instead, if you find yourself withdrawing with hurt feelings and vowing to not speak until your spouse makes you feel better about yourself, you are likely to find yourself isolating and pouting the next time this situation happens.

Whatever you defined as your most common ways of feeling and coping in Chapter 1, we know from brain research that it has happened that way to you a thousand times before. We also know that, if the pattern is left unchecked, you will feel and behave the same way again. It has become natural to you. You feel, think, and behave automatically when your buttons are pushed. Even if you hate the feelings and behaviors you engage in, your brain has become accustomed to the firing sequence. Just like the water from the melting snow finds its way to the crevasses and canyons naturally, so your brain will find these feelings and behaviors again and again. It is natural and easy. In fact, we know that the brain prefers these actions and behaviors because they are easy and comfortable.

In short, you have worn a rut in your brain. If you feel that you are unloved or unappreciated, then each time you are wronged you will feel it again. If you feel threatened, insecure, or unsafe, then every time a tentative situation comes up, you will likely have the same feelings. If your normal reactions are blaming others, shaming yourself, controlling others, or escaping pressure, you will likely find yourself resorting to the same methods again and again.

Now, if this seems like bad news, it is not. In fact, it is just the opposite of bad news because it confirms what we discussed in Chapter 1. When you have difficulty in relationships, you are not doing one hundred things wrong but instead are engaging in a basic pattern that is causing all the distress. The pattern is predictable and therefore you can recognize it and watch how it plays out again and again in your life. In other words, being so predictable means that you are more likely to be able to change and take the "old self" off and learn something new.

Abandoning an old pathway and creating a new one. The second important thing that the field of neuroscience has taught us over the past few years is that it takes intentional effort and much practice to form new connections between neurons. Think of it as moving into a new wilderness to cut a new pathway that is better than the old, worn-out trail that leads to the wrong place. Yes, it is much easier to travel on the pathway that is already there, but you will end up in the wrong place, doing the same things and feeling the same frustrating emotions.

It takes work to form a new habit, thought, behavior, or feeling. Your brain will feel it when we start telling you how to go about the process. You will say something like, "This is hard" or "This does not feel natural." Precisely. That is your brain telling you that there is already an old chain or pathway ready to be used that it prefers. It is your "old self" calling to you, begging you not to change.

This is the reason Scripture tells us that we need to put on the "new self." It is not easy, but it is the way of growth and change that will not only make you a better person but will also lead to your marriage and other relationships being in a better place. You have to realize that the same old Pain Cycle has led to problems and perhaps has put your marriage close to death. The same behavior is not good for you. It is time to realize that what comes naturally is not the best. It is time for a methodology to help you break that new ground in you brain.

This is about creating the new neural pathways in your brain that form the basis of the new self. We will teach you the structure, but you must hear us when we say that structure is only half of the work you will need to do. The other half of the work is practice. You will have to practice this "new self" behavior over and over again until your brain begins to recognize the pattern, process, and emotion as familiar. In other words, you are going to have to use the pathway enough until it wears a rut of its own!

No doubt you have heard the phrase "It has become second nature." That is what this process is about. What comes naturally to you is the "old self" and the first nature. This new ground that you are breaking is what we want you to practice until it becomes your "new self" and second nature. With practice, the new thoughts, emotions, and behaviors can become just as familiar and natural as the old way, with the difference that it will be good for you as an individual and good for your marriage and other relationships.

How much practice will it take? It is hard to say, but we think that if you can practice something every day for three months, you will learn it as a new habit. It does not mean that you will never go back to the old way, but it does mean that the new behavior will be familiar enough to you that you know exactly how to change and get back on track.

In January 2009, U.S. Airways flight 1549 smashed into a flock of geese just after leaving LaGuardia Airport in New York. Both engines were put out of commission and the plane was hopelessly crippled and going down. Everyone in the plane immediately knew the seriousness of the situation. For the passengers, their old, first natures told them to feel fear and panic. But the crew, and especially the pilot, Chesley B. "Sully" Sullenberger, reacted differently. They reacted according to their training.

Within seconds of the loss of the engines, Sully communicated with LaGuardia on landing options and, step by step, assessed the options of what he could do to land the plane. In the end he made the decision to land the plane on the Hudson River. He and his copilot worked through checklists to prepare the aircraft for the water landing, while the flight attendants in the back of the plane worked to prepare passengers. With almost unbelievable skill, Sully guided the plane down while keeping the nose slightly up and reducing the forward rate of motion to a survivable crash speed. You know the rest of the story. The crew ditched the plane in the Hudson River and all 155 people aboard the plane survived.

A miracle? In many ways, yes. But Sullenberger and his crew said over and over again that their training kicked in as soon as they realized the seriousness of the situation. They had been through similar scenarios over and over again in flight simulators that gave them the practice, skill, and expertise to land the plane. If they had done what just came naturally to their first nature, there would have been panic and likely 155 fewer souls here on earth. But because they had trained their second nature adequately, they immediately had brain pathways that could respond and solve the problem. In many ways, their second nature had now become as natural as the first. We believe that the flight landing was part miracle, but it was mostly a miracle of practice.

The apostle Paul, under the influence of the Holy Spirit and two thousand years before neuroscience, told us about this miraculous process of practice. It is about not being conformed to the old behavior but renewing and transforming the mind to adopt a new behavior. This new behavior can be learned, practiced, and commanded until it becomes as natural as anything you have ever learned well in your life.

Are you ready to learn the process? Let us get started.

The Four Steps

The passage from Ephesians 4 reveals a two-step process in this practice of renewing your mind: you take off the old and put on the new. The first two steps in our process are intended to help you first take off the old. The following two steps help you put on the new.

Remember from the review of how the brain works that the pull of the old thoughts, emotions, and behaviors is powerful and takes effort on your part to overcome. The first two steps then, are intended to let your brain know that you are fully knowledgeable of your old behaviors and your "tricks" in keeping those behaviors going.

STEP 1: Say what you feel.

This step has you call out how you are actually feeling. So to begin, review how you normally feel, as shown in **Exercise 1, page 16**. This is essential because, in the midst of a fight, you will be tempted to say things like, "I feel angry" or "I feel frustrated" or "I feel like leaving." Remember that all these phrases are representative of what you are doing right now and how you are coping with how you feel. It may be true that you are angry, but you are acting that way because you have had your old pain activated by feeling unloved, unwanted, controlled, or whatever it may be. Remember that these feelings are the ones that you most likely feel again and again, not only from your interactions with your spouse but also from a variety of relationships, including the ones in your family of origin. In many ways, this is about actualizing your real feelings. Instead of confusing your most basic and primary emotions with secondary actions like anger, guilt, shame, controlling, or escaping, you are accurately naming the true heart of emotion.

In our previous examples, Bill may think he feels like isolating and closing off, but in actuality he feels unaccepted and feels that he does not measure up. When he names his emotions, he is off to a good start.

And here's another thing. When we give the instruction, "Say what you feel," we truly mean to say it—say it out loud. This is based on current brain research. You see, your brain is able to sift through a huge number of thoughts, emotions, and actions in just a few seconds. With all this information coming at one time—sort of like looking at every card in the deck within ten seconds—it is no wonder that it gets confusing and you are tempted to go with the thought, emotion, or behavior you know best. But when you say what you feel out loud, you are actually moving the thoughts to a different part of your brain. Your brain hears what you are saying, and that process enables you to select and pay careful attention to it. Instead of a whole deck of cards, you are now dealing with two, three, or four cards—and dealing with them in a place where you can start your evaluation.

Your response to us might be, "You want me to say this out loud right when my partner and I are in a fight and out of the blue?" The answer is yes. Your partner will quickly recognize that you are working through your own process. If your spouse also reads this book, it will serve as a signal to him or her to start working the steps. But even if you are by yourself, express these things aloud. Saying them out loud stacks the cards in your favor, enabling you to change something that you are feeling and head in a different direction.

Whatever you listed in **Exercise 1, page 16**, as the way you feel, we want you to get those words programmed into your brain. Those are the descriptors of how you feel a good 85 to 95 percent of the time when you are distressed. You don't have to invent or look for how you feel every time, because you have already identified how you feel in **Exercise 1, page 16**. Getting it into your head means memorizing that list and practicing it over and over again through step 1. Say what you feel!

STEP 2: Say what you normally do.

Now that you have given your brain a fighting chance and let it actualize and realize how it feels, it is time to do some prediction of behavior. If you look back at **Exercise 3, page 22**, you will find those actions and behaviors that you normally take in order to cope with the feelings that you feel. Again, these actions and behaviors are very predictable and you will be doing some version of this coping 85 to 95 percent of the time when you are under stress or a conflict.

When we tell you, "Say what you normally do," we mean again to say it out loud. In our opinion, this is one of the most effective ways to short-circuit your "old self" behavior. When you say what you normally do in the way of coping or actions, you are actually predicting what you could do and remembering what you have done in the past. You know that these choices have not been good for you and have not been good for the relationship. When you say them out loud, it is as if you are confessing that you once again have the potential to take those destructive actions and the very things that have not worked for you in the past. Once again, you are naming your "tricks" to your brain in a format where you can hear them and think about them differently.

If you just keep this information to yourself and choose not to say it out loud, you will find yourself slipping into those same old destructive behaviors. You will find that once you start blaming others, shaming yourself, getting angry, judging, being sarcastic, withdrawing, pouting, running away, yelling, throwing things, falling apart, or whatever your coping action happens to be, it will be hard to stop until you have made a mess of things again. If you name it beforehand, your brain looks at the actions more as a choice, and it does not just slide into the behavior naturally.

We believe in you. We believe that if you can slow your brain down long enough to make a choice, you will make the choice the overwhelming majority of the time to continue with the steps and take off this "old self" behavior.

STEP 3: Say the truth.

Chances are, if you are emotionally aroused because you are hurt by what your spouse just did, angry at the way he or she behaved, or just plain anxious about what is going to happen next, you will experience the first two steps as doing little to calm your emotions. This is completely normal. In step 1, you are simply acknowledging the root of the primary emotion you feel. In step 2, you have merely informed yourself in a more objective way about the behavior you don't want to do. It is here in step 3 that we expect you to actually receive some emotional release.

When you say the truth, we want you to say the truth about yourself that you identified back in **Exercise 5, page 40**. Whenever you are dealing with the emotions that you normally feel when you are stressed, you are actually dealing with lies from the past about yourself and your situation. You may feel unloved. It is a lie. You may feel worthless. It is a lie. You may feel like a failure. It is a lie. You may feel that every situation you are in is unsafe. It is a lie. If you let yourself stay with the feelings of the "old self," you will in essence allow yourself to live in the lies. These lies will eventually prompt you to cope, which will take you back to your old destructive behaviors.

We don't want you to clamp down on your feelings that lead you to destructive actions, but instead we want you to confront them. When you say the truth out loud to yourself, you are giving yourself a message that is really a gift. It not only acknowledges what is true about you but also has the opportunity to replace the lies that you currently believe.

How do you make them more than just words you say? Remember our discussion in the previous chapter about the truth of who you are. If you will believe God through His Holy Spirit and His Word, and if you listen to your encouraging friends, mentors, and counselors, then these truths have a chance to become more than just words. You will emotionally begin to attach to the words because they produce feelings of peace within you.

You probably will have to say them more than once. You may have to take a few deep breaths when you say each truth. But if you will take the time to actually say the truths to yourself and allow the words to become powerful, you will likely notice that some of the tension will leave your body. You will find that the anxiety you felt just a few minutes before will begin leaving. You may notice that the furrow in your brow from all that anger that you were carrying eases. You will likely notice that your breathing becomes easier and you let go, heaving a relaxing sigh. The truth is an emotional elixir that leads you back into the Peace Cycle and gives you a glimpse of what your "new self" can feel like when it confronts emotions constructively. You will likely start recognizing this feeling connected to the truth as peace.

One warning about step 3: watch and regulate your emotions. Some folks will get into working the four steps and sound something like this: "How do I feel? I feel worthless, unappreciated, and like a failure. When I feel this way, what do I normally do? I normally get angry, negative, and attack. What is the truth? The truth is that you don't care about me and don't love me. The truth is that you are a jerk!" In other words, we often are still emotionally stimulated to the point where we are not ready to talk about the truth but instead want to use this step to comment on how our spouse is treating us poorly, is untrustworthy, or is hurtful. Of course this is not what step 3 is about.

If you find yourself saying something like the statements above, you need to cycle yourself back to step 1 and start again. You may need to say, "Again, what I feel is worthless, unappreciated, and like a failure. What I normally do when I feel that way is I get angry, negative, sarcastic, and attacking."

You may in fact have to back up to steps 1 and 2 many times before you find that you can actually say the truth and hear the truth. It is perfectly fine to have to repeat the steps again and again until they start making a difference. If you have to do steps 1 and 2 as many as ten times before you can say and believe the truth, then do them ten times. The point is that when you actually are able to say the truth to yourself, you will likely notice that it will shift where you are emotionally, and you will have a growing sense of peace instead of pain.

STEP 4: Say what you will do differently.

If you take the step to hear and start believing the truth, you will likely find yourself empowered to make a different behavioral choice. Instead of coping with those destructive feelings and lies, you will be able to understand the truth and look at what you can do differently. Those specific choices for you are found back in **Exercise 6, page 49**. Take a look at those behaviors that you identified and ingrain them in your heart's memory. These are the behaviors that will likely always be "winners" when it comes to your interactions with your spouse. As you use them, you will build a sense of accomplishment and growth.

Remember also that these behaviors are the very ones that contribute to a different emotional condition in your spouse. These actions and responses—when you use them in conjunction with your truth—will produce feelings in your spouse that reinforce who he or she is in God and the reality about the safety and trustworthiness of relationships. This builds into the process of the Peace Cycle, and you will likely find that your spouse starts behaving in ways that reinforce the truth in you.

IDEA
To Remember:

The Four Steps

Step 1: Say what you feel.

Step 2: Say what you normally do.

Step 3: Say the truth.

Step 4: Say what you will do differently.

Practice, Practice, Practice ... Success

The four steps to change in your marriage are not some magical formula. They are, in truth, just steps that should assist you in doing the hard work that is necessary to move yourself from the Pain Cycle into the Peace Cycle. It is a practical methodology of taking off the "old self" and putting on the "new self" right at the critical point where you need to interrupt the destructive feelings and behaviors that often take us over in relationships before we know what is happening to us.

We remind you again that in working through the four steps you may have to back up and start with step 1 several times. If you are in an intense situation with your spouse that causes fear, hurt, or stress, you both may need to cycle through the four steps many times within a ten-minute period to stay on track. But you can do this and you can actually move yourself from those old feelings and behaviors to a new position of truth and constructive action.

That's what Yolanda, the wife who called her marriage "hell," found out.

Yolanda was just about ready to light the torch of her anger as she was listening to Jody give a list of all the things that were wrong with the marriage. When Jody paused, though, Yolanda made a critical decision. "Okay, I'm going to try these four steps," she stated angrily. "Right now I am feeling powerless and like a failure! What I normally do when I feel that way is attack you with all the things that I think you do wrong and start justifying myself. I usually become more and more unreasonable as I blame. (Takes a deep breath.) But the truth is that I can control myself and I do have power. I am loved and I am wanted. (Much softer now.) So what I am going to do differently is, I want to take responsibility to change some of those things that I don't like about myself and use my power to suggest that we discuss how to solve some of these things constructively instead of getting mad about them."

Jody was stunned. He replied, "You are absolutely right on target." He worked through his four steps, and instead of the two of them ending up in a throw-down argument, they had a five-minute discussion and actually came up with two ideas for how they could get closer in their relationship.

After the interchange, Yolanda said, "I don't believe how much difference those steps made. I was all ready to go down the same direction and didn't want to do the steps at all, but I decided that I would give it a try just to prove it didn't work. It does work. I feel so different now."

You need to make the same discovery. Start by working through **Exercise 9**.

EXERCISE 9
Practicing the Four Steps

1. Think about the last situation, conflict, or fight you had with your spouse that caused distress or anxiety for either of you. Keeping this situation in mind, go through each of the four steps, saying aloud what you felt, what you did when you felt the way you did, what the truth is about you, and what you could have done that would have been more constructive.

2. Practice the four steps several times, focusing on the same scenario or others from the recent past. If it is comfortable or possible, get with your spouse and share what you discovered about your process in the four steps.

3. If comfortable or possible, take one of the items you identified as being more constructive in question 1 above and try to practice the behavior with your spouse.

The "Us" of the Relationship

You may look at these four steps and think, "If my spouse would do those four steps and stop doing his (or her) coping, I would certainly do my part and act differently." It is much easier for all of us to see what another person is doing incorrectly than to see it in ourselves. We are even sure that you see a good part of the Pain Cycle in your spouse accurately. The point is, however, that you must concentrate on changing yourself because you know the futility of trying to change another person.

If you are willing to practice and perfect the four steps, you have the potential to profoundly change your marital relationship, or your and your spouse's "us-ness." We've mentioned that term already. But what exactly is "us-ness"?

Many years ago, an old family therapist who had been married to his wife for more than fifty years mused, "You know, I love my wife. I would miss her terribly if she were to die. But as much as I would miss her if she were to die, I would miss what we are together more."

This "what we are together" is what we call "us." It is not just you as an individual or your spouse as an individual. You are not like two cats that have their tails tied together, thrown over a clothesline and left to fight it out. You are two people who have come together to form a third and brand-new identity. This new identity is your "us-ness."

"Us" has a personality of its own. It has its own likes and dislikes (things that you both enjoy doing together that you don't necessarily love as individuals). It has its own personality and predictability (such as knowing what each other will likely say next during a discussion or conflict). "Us" may be invisible, but it indeed is a separate identity from you as an individual or your spouse as an individual.

"Us" is much like a child that comes from a marriage. The child may have half of the genetic material from the father and half from the mother, but the genetic code combines to make a whole new person. What your children represent in terms of your physical codes producing a brand-new third person, your "us-ness" represents in terms of your emotional codes producing a third identity.

You and your spouse's "us" has a rhythm, personality, and life of its own. But like a child, it is kept alive and nurtured by the parents. Spouses need to see their "us-ness" much as they see themselves as responsible for the well-being of a child. If spouses do not care for and nurture their "us," it will fail to grow and will eventually die.

You don't hear parents declare, "I want our child to eat well because it is the best for me. I want our child to do well in school because it is best for me." They want their child to eat well and do well in school because it is in the best interest of the child. The same is true with our "us-ness." If we are battling in our marriages over who is going to win or lose in a fight between spouses, we are failing to see that we need to look out for the best interest of "us."

If we let this perspective soak in a bit, it has the potential to change our behavior radically. Instead of seeing my feelings, my thoughts, and my behavior as being in a competition with my spouse, I have the opportunity to turn my feelings, thoughts, and behaviors toward what will be in the best interest of our "us-ness" in the same way that two parents look out for the best interest of a child. In other words, it changes a framework of competition to one of cooperation.

What does this have to do with staying on your side of the fence and working on your own four steps and your own Peace Cycle? When you take the responsibility to change yourself and not focus on changing your spouse, you automatically take away half of the old Pain Cycle. With half of the Pain Cycle gone, and at least half of the Peace Cycle trying to operate in the relationship, you will by definition change the relationship. As you become healthier, you will be better at interacting in nondestructive and constructive ways in the relationship.

Will this change your spouse? It certainly will change the situation for your spouse, even though it will not directly change him or her. But what it will change most is what you and your spouse are together. It will create a healthier "us" in your relationship. It is certainly better for both spouses to work on themselves simultaneously to improve the relationship. In the words of Proverbs 27:17, *"As iron sharpens iron, so one man sharpens another."* But even if you feel like your spouse is not trying as hard as you, or maybe not even trying at all, it is important to remember that you have the power to change yourself and at least part of your "us-ness."

If you and your spouse are on the same page about weeding out the "old self" behavior and getting out of the Pain Cycle, then it is important to remember that you will often come across times when stopping the old behavior will not be perfect. Many times, you both may fall right back into the old patterns and escalate anxiety, anger, or destructive actions. This is normal, because none of us will get out of our old destructive pattern perfectly.

After you realize that you fell into the same old pattern, don't just give up and say this program didn't work. Go back to the cycle that you detailed in Day 1 and say what happened and what you observed in retrospect. Almost certainly, you will be able to see exactly the points where you both got trapped into the old feelings and coping behaviors. This identification helps make it more likely that the next time it occurs you will be able to interrupt the cycle while it is happening. Even if you feel as if you failed at getting out of the Pain Cycle this time, don't be discouraged but instead review the patterns.

You will do better if you keep the Pain Cycle and Peace Cycle in front of you. Perhaps you could make a larger version of your Pain and Peace Cycles and put them up on the wall of your bedroom, your closet, or even your refrigerator. When you and your spouse find yourselves in the old pain, go to the place where you have your cycles and finish your discussion there. You will find that you quickly are both staring at the old feelings and behaviors and pressing one another toward the four steps and getting into the Peace Cycle. You can also use the same type of process by making miniature copies of your Pain and Peace Cycles and carrying them with you in your purse or wallet. Anything that you can do to keep these cycles in front of you, especially when you are emotionally activated, will increase the likelihood that you will be able to work the four steps and make the transition in taking off the old and putting on the new.

IDEA
To Remember:

Your marriage is an "us-ness" that is more than just what you and your spouse are individually. Take care of your "us."

Another effective strategy in working with your spouse to change "us" is to take a timeout for ten minutes when you are trapped in the Pain Cycle. During that ten minutes, you and your spouse should each go and spend time looking over the Pain Cycle, the Peace Cycle, and the four steps. At the end of the ten minutes, the two of you should come back together and see if you can stay in the Peace Cycle. If you escalate or get upset again, call another timeout and both go and review the cycles and steps once again. If you do this process three times with three timeouts and still cannot work yourselves into a better place, you may need to take a longer timeout or seek the help of a trained counselor. But we believe that, for the overwhelming majority of times, you and your spouse will be able to work yourselves out of the Pain Cycle and into the Peace Cycle after one timeout.

Finally, don't forget what we have taught you about the brain. You will learn how to move from the Pain to Peace Cycle using the four steps only by practice, practice, and more practice.

We know that working the four steps and the cycles can be tiresome, but continued effort makes all the difference in the world. *"Let us not become weary in doing good, for at the proper time we will reap a harvest if we do not give up"* (Galatians 6:9).

**IDEA
To Remember:**

*When you and your spouse are in the
Pain Cycle and cannot seem to quit, take
a purposeful ten-minute timeout.*

For Reflection

1. Reflect on moments when the truth about who you are has soaked in and impacted the way you felt. At those times, what do you notice about your emotions? What do you notice about the way your body felt and reacted?

2. Think about your brain and the process it will take in order to transform the old self into the new self. Ask God to help you as you endeavor to make this change real in your life.

3. Meditate on the following verse: *"If you have any encouragement from being united with Christ, if any comfort from his love, if any fellowship with the Spirit, if any tenderness and compassion, then make my joy complete by being like-minded, having the same love, being one in spirit and purpose. Do nothing out of selfish ambition or vain conceit, but in humility consider others better than yourselves. Each of you should look not only to your own interests, but also to the interests of others"* (Philippians 2:1-4).

4. From the *5 Days to a New Marriage* App: **Day 3**, complete and practice the Four Steps to internalize the process of emotional regulation. *Download the 5 Days to a New Marriage app from your App Store, search "New Marriage."*

A Different Future

Relaunching to a New Marriage

Day 4

If you have peace in your marriage, you are going to find that as a couple you are going to do amazing things. All of the energy and effort that have been consumed in arguments, conflicts, and separation now have the potential of being freed up to put to constructive use in your marriage. Day 4 is about helping you use that energy for the benefit of your partnership, or your "us-ness." From this connected position, you can grow your "us-ness" by tapping into the power of four critical processes: capitalizing on strengths, problem-solving, forgiving each other, and developing a vision.

We want you to focus on a new beginning for your marriage, or a relaunch of your marriage. Relaunch may seem like a silly word. As a matter of fact, the spellchecker keeps wanting to reject it. The "re" part of the word indicates that this is the second time, whereas most of us never thought much about our "us-ness" the first time around.

Think back to your wedding day. That probably means friends, family, flowers, a ceremony, and some kind of celebration. You were probably excited and nervous about what this new life together was going to be like. In the midst of all that hoopla, it's unlikely you were thinking about what your marriage team, or your "us-ness," was going to be about. You probably weren't thinking things like: "What is our personality as a couple? What are our goals together? How are we going to nurture what we are together?" And the fact that you did not consider these questions may be part of the reason you got off track in the first place.

Anything in life that we neglect or fail to pay attention to will ultimately get worse with time. Ignore an infection in your body, and it will eventually take over and cost you a limb or your life. Fail to pay attention to what your toddlers are up to, and within seconds they will spill, injure, or destroy something. Similarly, neglect your "us-ness," and marriage will become stagnant, distant, and divided.

And that gets to the heart of the matter. You stood at an altar and made a covenant to be united, together, on the same team. Yet, over time, your team has taken some hits and you have turned on each other. A house divided against itself cannot stand. A marriage divided against itself cannot succeed.

Your marriage has an enemy—call him Satan, the world, the dark side, or whatever you choose—that wants to see you fail. The goal of the enemy is to divide you and turn you against each other. That's the bad news. But there is good news: You have a teammate who is more powerful than any enemy. The Lord wants to see you succeed. And the enemy cannot stand against Him.

Ecclesiastes 4:12 says, *"Though one may be overpowered, two can defend themselves. A cord of three strands is not quickly broken,"* and that's how it is for you. With your spouse on your side, the two of you can defend yourselves. And united to your spouse with God on your side, you can do anything.

In essence, to function like an "us-ness," you have to partner with one another to accomplish things that neither of you could pull off alone. This relaunch of your "us" gives you the unique opportunity to get more right in your marriage than you ever thought possible.

The Strengths Each One Brings

Great teams are made up of different people bringing their individual talents together for a common goal. The same applies to your marital "us-ness." You and your spouse are different, and that is a good thing. You both were designed by God with unique strengths, gifts, talents, and abilities that can make a tremendous difference in the world. These strengths have been with you from birth, but they often take time to discover, nurture, and develop. You will recognize a good number of these strengths from the Bible.

"The fruit of the Spirit is love, joy, peace, patience, kindness, goodness, faithfulness, gentleness and self-control. Against such things there is no law." (Galatians 5:22-23)

"In Christ we who are many form one body, and each member belongs to all the others. We have different gifts, according to the grace given us. If a man's gift is prophesying, let him use it in proportion to his faith. If it is serving, let him serve; if it is teaching, let him teach; if it is encouraging, let him encourage; if it is contributing to the needs of others, let him give generously, if it is leadership, let him govern diligently; if it is showing mercy, let him do it cheerfully." (Romans 12:5-8)

The beauty of operating in the truth about how you are loved by God and how God is trustworthy is that it frees you to behave in line with the natural gifts, talents, strengths, and traits that God has specifically designed in you. Those gifted in empathy are able to show care for their spouse. Those gifted in communication are free to slow down and listen. Those gifted in wisdom are able to apply truth in ways that change the interactions with their spouse for the better. These are just a few of the gifts.

One key to remember is that you cannot possibly possess all of these strengths. You have only the ones God gave you. That is why your marital "us-ness" is so important. Your spouse brings a different set of strengths to the marriage. When operating in his or her truth, your spouse is free to express the gifts and talents that God designed in him or her. Your different gifts can complement each other, and you can achieve things as a couple that would never have been possible if you were alone. Through time, hard work, and experience, you can learn to balance your strengths to enhance your "us-ness." You can even find ways to call out the gifts you see in your spouse and then create a space and opportunities for your spouse to utilize his or her unique talents and abilities. The winner in this arrangement is your "us-ness."

Coming Up with Solutions Together

Understanding and operating in your unique strengths will greatly improve your marital "us-ness." Even in the best teams, however, there is sometimes conflict. Conflict in and of itself is not bad, because it reflects the struggle of two individuals to conform to an "us-ness" for the good of the marriage. In the past, conflict has probably driven you into your Pain Cycle, so you may have come to the wrong conclusion: that conflict is to be avoided at all costs. Good teams, however, figure out how to address their differences head-on and find productive resolutions for the good of the "us." Therefore, the second process you want to master for the sake of your "us-ness" is problem solving.

Putting your "us-ness" ahead of your individual desires is really hard when you don't like your spouse or when you don't agree on something. Disagreements, disputes, arguments, and conflict are a natural part of any earthly relationship. However, most married couples make significant mistakes in their conflicts by spending an inordinate amount of time trying to win an argument, prove a point, assign blame, or be "right." Does that sound like your conflicts?

In those moments, you turn against your teammate and your "us-ness" gets pushed to the background. It would be like playing doubles tennis and telling your partner that he is no good, thus demoralizing him and causing him to leave the court. In that scenario, you might prove your point to your tennis partner, but you are now left to play the two opponents by yourself. In essence, your team has been weakened when you attack your partner. In doubles tennis, you win the match or lose the match together. There is no way for one partner to win and the other to lose.

Marriage is like doubles tennis. You either win together or lose together. And if either of you feels as if you are constantly losing, then your team, or your "us," is the one really taking the loss.

How do you choose to do what is good for the team, or "us," in moments like this? The fact is, you will not be able to unless you have a process in place that resolves issues while emphasizing the importance of your marital "us-ness." Couples without a system for resolving conflict are destined to stay locked in power struggles and fights that erode trust, damage each other, and ultimately destroy their marriage. But there is good news: a few simple steps can get you on the right track to solving problems as a team.

There are a wide variety of problem-solving steps that you can find in the literature out there, from the PREP model (Markman, Stanley, and Blumberg) to the PAIRS model (DeMaria and Hannah) to the DNA for Relationships model (Smalley and Paul). Our steps below are not much different from some of these, but they are simple ones that we have found helpful in working with couples on solving problems and staying focused on their "us-ness." First, make sure that you are operating out of your Peace Cycle and not harming one another in your Pain Cycle. Then, secure in your truth, read about these steps and watch how our couple, Bill and Sandy, applied them to resolve a difficult decision they faced.

"Us" Problem-Solving Step 1

Commit to stay together in the process and on the solution. When there is a problem to be solved, we naturally have our individual outlooks and opinions that tell us what needs to happen. We usually try to force our individual solutions onto our spouse. But if you are going to stay focused in problem solving, what you think individually is not so important. What is important is teaching yourselves and learning how to think together out of your marital "us-ness." Coming to a problem and thinking, "How do we choose a solution that is good for our marriage?" is totally different from saying, "This is how I think we should solve this problem" or "This is how I demand we solve it because I know that I am right."

Let's be clear on one thing. You may think you know what is best in terms of how to spend the money, raise the kids, relate to in-laws, or establish the frequency of sex, but you do not. What we have learned through the years is that God is much more interested in your learning how to stay together through a problem than in your solving the problem. The sooner you learn and commit to staying together in the process and the solution, the sooner you will see changes in the way you avoid conflicts and build strength in your team.

Like teammates in a basketball game fighting for a rebound, someone needs to yell, "We are on the same team!" before the ball bounces out of bounds. Once you both acknowledge that attacking each other is only going to result in a loss for your team, you can begin figuring out how you both can stay on the ball and move on to the next step.

Remember Bill and Sandy, whom we first met in Chapter 1? They made significant improvements in their marriage by understanding their Pain and Peace Cycles and by working the steps to relate to each other in a more loving away. Even with all that, however, they still have conflicts they cannot resolve.

One of these is that Bill really wants Sandy to home-school their five-year-old daughter. Sandy is dead set against this idea because public school had been good enough for her and it is good enough for her daughter. Every time they discuss the issue, they end up turning on each other in a loud argument and often move into their Pain Cycle.

But then they agree to try to resolve this issue by choosing a solution together and staying an "us" through the process. So they begin their discussion by acknowledging that working together is the most important thing. They agree that they are not just looking for what is in the best interests of their daughter, but they are also looking out for what is best for their "us-ness."

"Us" Problem-Solving Step 2:

Talk about possible solutions. Life forces choices, and choices often must be made in a timely fashion. When we feel the pressure of making a decision or choosing a solution, we often only focus on our own solution and consider why it is better than our spouse's solution. Seldom do we think about the possible solutions that are good for our team and "us." So we want to communicate to you that looking at the problem from different perspectives and considering other possible solutions will increase the likelihood that you and your spouse will find solutions together. Remember that winning individually while your spouse loses means that your "us-ness" loses. Your way is not the best way for your "us" unless the "us" feels good about it.

It is usually best in thinking about the possible solutions to listen more than you speak. Be sincere in your effort to not only speak about what you think but also really look for other ideas that might have value in solving the problem. Listen to your spouse and his or her reasoning. Write down the possible solutions and make sure that you and your spouse have given every solution some consideration.

In Bill and Sandy's case, they calmly talk about possible solutions for their daughter's schooling, being careful not to use the opportunity to lobby for the solution that each one thinks best. They find themselves not only pointing out positive aspects of other solutions but also acknowledging weaknesses and negatives in their own individual solutions.

Since this context of listening to solutions builds an opportunity to safely share what's really going on in each other's hearts, Bill and Sandy open up on a new level. Sandy shares her concerns that she is not adequately prepared to teach their daughter to read. She wants the best for their daughter, and Sandy does not feel equipped to provide it. Bill hears her feelings instead of just wanting to prove her wrong. Sandy actually feels understood, and then she is eager to listen to Bill. He states that his big concern is not really the education itself but the values their daughter would be exposed to in the public school. He wants his little girl to be in a safe and nurturing environment. Sandy cries as she sees the "daddy's heart" in her husband.

At the completion of this step, they still do not know what to do with their daughter's education, but they certainly feel a higher level of understanding and connection and have the options out on the table.

"Us" Problem-Solving Step 3:

Pray together. Prayer is an amazing tool in marriage. Research overwhelmingly supports the axiom that "couples who pray together, stay together." Prayer will do two things for your teamwork.

First, prayer will enable you to hear God's opinion on the decision you are trying to make. Of course, if you and your spouse are fighting over what color to paint the bedroom, God may not really care! But if you are trying to make a major life decision, such as where to live or whether to have kids, you would certainly want input from the God who knows the plans He has for you (Jeremiah 29:11).

Second, and possibly even more important, praying together will become a uniting act for you. After all, you rarely see two adversaries stop to pray with and for each other. On the contrary, praying with someone joins and connects you. It is a recommitment that you are on the same team looking for a common solution.

Bill and Sandy pray together once a day for a week about what to do with their daughter's schooling. They never hear a clear answer from God, but they agree that they feel more connected than ever before regarding the topic at hand.

"Us" Problem-Solving Step 4:

Pick a solution. If you go through the first three steps, you will likely start feeling the truth that staying together as a couple is much more important than "winning" any particular point on how to solve the problem. You will likely start seeing that there are merits and problems with all solutions. So how do you come to a solution? Pick one.

It may be something new that you had never thought of before engaging these steps, or it may be something that your spouse wanted to do from the very beginning. The important thing is that at this point in the process you are both agreeing that this is the "us" decision you are going to employ. You agree that it is a team decision for which you both take full responsibility. It is no longer your decision or my decision, but it is our decision together. You will win or lose together with this decision, so both of you should be equally committed to implementing and executing the decision wholeheartedly. Make it happen.

After following all the steps, Bill and Sandy choose the public school option. Sandy had originally suggested this, but now it feels different. Bill is on board and feels good about the decision. In their research, Bill found out that the principal of the local public school is a Christian woman who is serious about her faith and values. Sandy is glad that a professional teacher will be teaching their daughter to read. On the same team and in agreement, they take their daughter to the local elementary school.

"Us" Problem-Solving Step 5:

Be willing to choose a different solution if necessary. Here is a big truth about problem solving: your solutions may not work. But the good news about this is that if you have remained on the same team and tried to do what was best for your "us," it is easier to revisit the solution that did not work and make a different choice. The process did not fail you; only your choice failed. Rework the process and pick a different solution. Start over with the teamwork steps and choose another option that you both agree will serve your "us-ness" and for which you can both be responsible. The victory is in being on the same team even if your decisions or choices sometimes do not work out.

The decision Bill and Sandy made was a big mistake. There are thirty kids in their daughter's class, and the teacher is overwhelmed. Had they not used the problem-solving process, you can guess what would be happening. Bill would be strutting around telling Sandy how he knew all along this was a bad idea and she should have just listened to him. But their conversation is not like that at all. They agree on the solution. The "us" made a mistake, and the "us" can work together to fix it. They rework the steps and choose a private school close to their home. Their daughter thrives in the nurturing environment. Bill and Sandy prevail as a team.

EXERCISE 10
Using the "Us" Problem-Solving Steps

1. Think of a conflict that you and your spouse have been unable to resolve. Agree with your spouse to work the "Us" Problem-Solving Steps to seek a resolution. If needed, ask another trusted couple to help you work through the steps. You can also refer back to the Bill and Sandy story in this Chapter for guidance.

2. Discuss what you learned about the process. Discuss how it affected your "us-ness."

Letting Go and Forgiving

Couples who capitalize on their strengths and problem-solve effectively together are nurturing their "us-ness." They honor and value each other's opinions, seek to understand as much as be understood, and work to find solutions that are beneficial to the marriage and not just themselves. The process of problem solving is extremely successful for couples resolving conflict in the here-and-now. However, some of the conflict in your marriage is tied to past wounds and hurts that you and your spouse inflicted on each other. Teamwork won't heal the past, but there is a second powerful process that can help in this area: forgiveness.

You have choices when you consider this question: "What am I going to do with my old hurt inflicted by my spouse?" You can hold on to it, use it against your spouse, let it justify protecting yourself, and keep yourself tied to it forever. Or you can do something about it. You can get to the heart of the matter and employ forgiveness. If you choose the second path, the following steps will help you unleash the power of forgiveness.

> # IDEA
> ## To Remember:
>
> *The process of forgiveness will free you from the power of past hurts.*

Forgiveness Step 1:

Acknowledge that you have been hurt. This first step seems simple and straight-forward because it is. You must admit that you have been hurt. Start by yourself. You do not have to wait for your spouse to come and ask for forgiveness. He or she may or may not be willing to participate, but the forgiveness is not really for that person. It is for you and your healing. It is eventually for your relationship and the "us-ness." God implores you to forgive for your own sake because He does not want you tied to old hurts.

Forgiveness Step 2:

Give yourself room to feel. Identify the emotions you have (pain, disappointment, anger, sadness, and so on). Don't ignore or stuff your feelings. Don't judge your own feelings as stupid or irrational. Don't justify your spouse's behavior to minimize your hurt. Give your heart the room it needs to grieve and feel.

The spouse whose partner has committed adultery needs to give himself or herself space to hurt and be upset. It will do no good in the long run to suck it up and act tough or to blame oneself for a spouse's immoral behaviors ("He had an affair because I was not meeting his needs"). The victim of an affair—or any other offense, for that matter—needs to give himself or herself the freedom to feel the hurt.

Forgiveness Step 3:

Take care of yourself. Violations tend to deplete one's energy. So get recharged. Take some time for yourself. Remind yourself of the truth about who you are. Get your heart reengaged in life, not protected behind walls. Pray for God to bring you the comfort you need. This most often takes some time and may take some space.

Forgiveness Step 4:

Forgive from the heart. From a healthy, recharged place, you are ready to forgive. Do it and mean it.

Why go through this process when you could have just said, "I forgive you," a long time ago? You do this because the Bible is specific here. Jesus, for example, said, *"This is how my heavenly Father will treat each of you unless you forgive your brother from your heart"* (Matthew 18:35, emphasis added).

Forgiveness is too powerful a tool for mere lip service. You have to dig into the depths of your heart, experience the feelings, and reengage emotionally to truly forgive. If you do, then you will be free indeed. Your heart will be clean. You will no longer be tied to your spouse's words and actions from the past.

A few questions are worth clarifying in the area of forgiveness.

1. How long should the process of forgiveness take?

The answer varies depending on your experience with the process and the degree of offense you are dealing with. Your spouse giving you an evil look could take forty-five seconds to forgive. Working through infidelity and its ramifications could take months. Don't put a time limit on yourself. Just be true to the steps.

2. Should I tell my spouse that I forgive him or her?

That one is up to you and the condition of your marriage. You may want to tell your spouse, or you may just want to let him or her experience the new way of interacting that comes with your freedom.

3. What if I have gone through the entire process and I still can't forget what my spouse did to me?

Contrary to popular opinion, forgiveness is not the same as forgetting. There are some things you will never forget, and that is okay. You just want to forgive so that the memories don't have the same power over you as before forgiving.

4. Does this mean that I have to trust him (or her)?

No. Forgiveness and trust are separate processes. God commands you to forgive because He does not want you tied to someone else's poor behavior. God does not command you to trust, because that is dependent on the other person. You want to trust, but your spouse must prove trustworthy. You have to determine if it is a safe place for you to open your heart.

5. What if I have done some things to hurt my spouse?

If you recognize this, don't wait for your spouse to work through this process on his or her own. Go and ask for forgiveness. It will make it easier on your spouse as he or she proceeds through the steps, and it will go a long way to proving that you are trustworthy.

EXERCISE 11
Using the Forgiveness Steps

1. Are there some unresolved past hurts that you have not forgiven? List them. They may be from your spouse or anyone else in your life. Can you see how these past issues are still affecting you today?

_____

_____

2. Work through the forgiveness process steps outlined above. Ask God to help you every step of the way.

Identifying a Vision for Your "Us"

Is the value of your marital "us-ness" becoming clearer to you now? We hope so. Making space for each other's strengths will make you stronger. Problem-solving during conflict will help you over the inevitable bumps in the relationship. Forgiveness will release you from the energy-draining power of past hurts and offenses.

With all that you have been through and all you have applied from this book, you are ready for something totally new. Just as you were able to personally put off your old self and put on the new in Day 3, so you are now ready to do the same with your marriage. You do not have to go back to your old marriage. This is not a book to help you survive the bad marriage you have by applying a few new tools. This is about total transformation. Couples who go through as much as you have deserve something different—something better. You get to redefine your marital "us-ness."

The third process worth tapping into to strengthen your "us-ness," then, is the development of vision. What do you want your new marriage to look like? What are the desires of your heart for this relationship? What does God want from the two of you as a team?

The Bible tells us, *"Where there is no vision, the people perish"* (Proverbs 29:18, KJV). Likewise, without a vision for a new marriage, your efforts to change will fail. In contrast, a true vision for your relationship can revitalize and energize your life. Vision provides the motivation for significant accomplishment. Vision allows you to recalibrate your expectations, hopes, and dreams. Vision puts you on God's course for your marriage and family.

Having a vision unleashes a powerful positive process in your marriage. Speaking at a men's conference in Atlanta several years ago, James Rawls said that vision ignites the passion inside us that fuels the discipline it takes to be successful.

- Vision ignites passion. Athletes create a vision in their minds of themselves accomplishing a great victory, and this vision energizes, motivates, and excites them. Your marriage could use some passion. Unleash it by creating a vision you can both get excited about.

- Passion fuels discipline. Athletes' visions ignite passion that fuels their disciplined efforts to practice and push their bodies beyond normal limits. Similarly, discipline will be required to make the changes suggested in this book. Fuel the needed discipline with the passion ignited from a clear vision of where your marriage could be.

If this sounds like something you can do, then a turnaround lies just ahead. And in a way, it will get you back to where you always wanted to be.

After all, you started out with high hopes for a marriage filled with romance, excitement, and adventure. But then, all too soon, the reality of the struggles of life and relationships came along. You know them: bills and babies, traumas and trials, fights and fears. You quickly learned to abandon your dreams and adjust your expectations so as not to be let down.

Having abandoned your dreams for what your marriage could be, you settled for what you had. Rather than seeking greatness in your most important earthly relationship, you settled for good, okay, or—worse yet—tolerable. In settling, you ended up with a marriage that lacked vision, direction, and passion.

But things can be different. You have a new set of insights and tools to apply to your life and relationship. You do not have to settle. Begin to think about what your new marriage (with your current spouse) could look like. Why shouldn't your marriage be better? Dream it. Describe it. Discuss it with your wife or husband. Write it down. Ask God to help you.

Vision is simply the ability to see, but not everyone is good at "seeing" (imagining) what their marriage could look like, especially if there is a history of hurt and disappointment. So if you find yourself having trouble with developing a vision for your marriage, think about what you want others to see when they look at your marriage. Still another way to consider the question is to look at what you want to be the core characteristics of your marital "us-ness."

One more time, let's refer to Bill and Sandy. They were able to work this process for their good. Now they have a new marriage. They understand their past unhealthy patterns and have converted them to a new Peace Cycle. But they did not stop there. They created a vision for what they wanted their marriage to look like characterized by respect and positivity. They continue to employ teamwork to resolve conflicts and they are quick to forgive. Together, they have relaunched their marriage to a place they had stopped believing they could reach.

That can be your story. You deserve a relaunch. Don't go alone. Rely on the time-tested principles presented in this chapter. And, more importantly, trust in the God who inspired them. As we have been saying all along: you can do this!

IDEA
To Remember:

Vision allows you to see the possibility of a "new" future with your spouse.

Day 4

EXERCISE 12
Establishing a Vision for Your New Marriage

1. Look at the following list and circle two or three traits that you would want as core values in your "new" marriage. Write them down.

Freedom	Trust	Generosity	Teamwork
Respect	Adventure	Health	Tradition
Learning	Growth	Individuality	Wisdom
Intimacy	Perseverance	Integrity	Commitment
Safety	Creativity	Loyalty	Communication
Encouragement	Courage	Hospitality	Compassion
Truth	Honesty	Resourceful-	Empathy
Acceptance	Excellence	ness	Unity
Honor	Harmony	Sacrifice	
Authenticity	Adaptability	Service	
Faith	Fun	Simplicity	

2. Discuss your choices with your spouse. See if the two of you can both agree on three or four values that would contribute to a great "new" marriage.

_____

_____

For Reflection

1. Contrast the feelings of being on the same team versus being turned against your teammate. How freeing would it be to feel like you had a teammate pulling in the same direction as you—mutually seeking to grow your marital "us-ness"?

2. Which of the problem-solving steps do you usually get stuck on? What can you commit to doing differently when you get to that point next time?

3. What old offenses and hurts do you continue to carry around in your marriage? What is stopping you from working through the process of forgiveness? Pray for God to empower you to work through the forgiveness process.

4. Is it scary to allow yourself to have a vision about the possibility of a new marriage with your spouse? Acknowledge this to God—and even your spouse, if you feel safe enough. Let yourself begin to dream and have vision again. What do you want this marriage to look like?

5. From the *5 Days to a New Marriage* App: **Day 4**, begin to apply the Five Steps for Problem Solving with your spouse. *Download the 5 Days to a New Marriage app from your App Store, search "New Marriage."*

Your New Marriage—Forever

Understanding Where to Go From Here

Day

5

The previous chapters represent four days to make big changes—changes that can save your marriage, transform your marriage, take your marriage where you always dreamed it could go. But can it really be that simple? The truth is, no. It really is not that simple. It really is that hard. And that is why we are talking to you here on Day 5.

Everything that you have read here represents fairly simple concepts, but putting simple things into practice is often quite difficult. We know that this process works because we have seen couple after couple come to an understanding of their pain, their truth, and how to make it possible to live in the truth. Some of these folks are simple-minded and of humble origins, while some are among the smartest and most accomplished people we have ever met. Almost all understand the process equally because it is simple. But only the couples who are willing to take on the hard work of change—the day-in-and-day-out practice of these simple ideas—are the ones who revolutionize their marriages. The material is simple, but the work that you must keep at is hard.

So, how do you live out this change? If you work through the first four days, close the book, and say, "That was very helpful," then you will likely see marginal benefits. If, however, on Day 5 you practice what you learned on Day 1 through Day 4, you will move incrementally in a positive direction. If you continue practicing what you learned on Day 1 through Day 4 for a week, you will notice that the ideas and steps become much clearer and easier. If you stick with it for three weeks, you will discover that the more issues you confront with this process, the more powerful the process becomes in resolving conflict, solving problems, and forging a new intimacy between you and your spouse. And if you practice these strategies and exercises for three months, you will find that they become almost second nature to you and that your marriage cannot go back to the old way of functioning. When you have slip-ups and go back to the Pain Cycle, you will know how to get yourself back on track.

In other words, you need to go over these exercises again and again until they are so clear to you that they are imprinted on your heart. Keep this book near at hand and refer back to your cycles again and again. Review your truths and the behaviors that will always be winners for you. Say the four steps until you can recognize the process in the midst of even the most heated conflict, and commit yourself to live in the truth. For every problem that comes up in your relationship, commit to work the problem-solving steps until you and your spouse reach agreement. Forgive and forgive again. Don't stop dreaming and envisioning what your marriage can become.

You can do this. We are telling you that from Day 5 until "death do you part" you have the skills to practice until they become a natural way of living. If you live what you have learned, you will have that loving, trustworthy, and intimate marriage you long for.

The Next Step

How can you keep yourself on track? One effective way to learn and keep going with this process is to teach others the process. You can do this by following the directions in the *Five Days to a New Marriage Small-Group Leader's Guide* and utilizing the DVD training material. You may feel fearful and incompetent at moving someone else or a group through the process, but simply find another couple or couples you care about and share with them what this process has meant to you. Tell them that as a favor to help you learn and make the process real, you would like to lead them through this book so that you and your spouse can continue to practice the principles. It does not matter if the couple or couples you choose have a great marriage or a struggling marriage; force yourself to take at least one couple through the process of discovering the Pain Cycle, the Peace Cycle, and the four steps to change in the marital relationship. Teach them and remind yourself how to solve problems, forgive, and create vision: a new marriage.

You are doing this sharing to keep your own marriage on track. But, of course, you will also find that you might help another struggling marriage get back on course. Or you might be assisting a marriage that is already good to become great.

Keep your Peace and Pain Cycles in a prominent place, where you can use them to short-circuit conflicts. When your neighbors and family inquire about these cycles, explain what they mean and how they work in your marriage. You will find that, not only will people be interested in what you are sharing, but soon they will be expressing a desire to learn the same types of things about their relationships.

Alcoholics Anonymous has many simple philosophies that have been helpful to millions. One such helpful idea is that AA is "one drunk helping another drunk stay sober." All of us who have struggles in our marital relationship will quickly notice the same truth. When we reach out to some other couple and teach them how to improve their relationship using this simple process, we are not only helping them but also helping ourselves keep our marriage on track.

You need to help others for the sake of your own marriage.

More Help

Perhaps you are convinced that this material speaks to you, but you just cannot seem to understand how to make it real in your life. Maybe when you think about your own pain, it becomes overwhelming to you and you can't sort it out. Maybe you want to put this to use but can't seem to get your spouse to work on the process with you. And maybe you are not quite sure how to put the process into practice yourself. Whatever the reason, there are situations where a skilled counselor or therapist can be of some help to you.

One option is to schedule an intensive session at the place where this material was developed and used to help couples. The Hideaway Experience is located on the rim of a beautiful canyon in the heart of West Texas. In a setting that is sequestered, you find lodging and service that is as comfortable and secure as a loving home. Four couples come to The Hideaway for four days at a time and work through the process you have read about here under the guidance of two trained counselors or therapists. These professionals know how to help you understand your pain, find your truth, practice the new-self process, and formulate forgiveness and teamwork. In addition, a team of people who care about marriage pray for you and your spouse. In four days at The Hideaway Experience, you can get the kind of counsel and attention that would take months in traditional weekly therapy. To learn more, go online to *www.thehideawayexperience.com*.

Although The Hideaway Experience is the place where the material outlined in this book began and is practiced, there are similar marital intensive programs located in different parts of the country. These intensive programs help because they allow you and your spouse to focus on the marriage and develop some new patterns quickly to address the pain and distress you may be feeling. Any place that will provide you and your spouse with sequestering, focus, and a trained therapist can be a tremendous help to your relationship.

There also is the resource of a local counselor or therapist in your area. Such a professional will usually see you and your spouse on a weekly basis, and he or she can be of tremendous help in moving you and your marriage to a better place. It is always helpful to find a professional who believes in the value of marriage and uses techniques and practices that have helped other marriages. Ask those you trust—friends, pastors, and other couples—the name of a professional whom they can recommend.

Marriage can be a fulfilling and wonderful journey. Whether it is through this book, a marital-intensive program, enrichment programs, or work with a counselor or therapist, you can move your marriage to a better place. For that matter, you can have a brand-new marriage. Even if you have tried before and not been successful, your work to have a satisfying and growing relationship is worth the effort and is an honorable endeavor.

You can do this!

For Reflection

1. From the *5 Days to a New Marriage* App: **Day 5**, Use the Values, Vision, Quiz tools to foster intentional Self-Care for you and your marriage. *Download the 5 Days to a New Marriage app from your App Store, search "New Marriage."*

Acknowledgments

This book comes from a collaboration of the therapists and proprietors of The Hideaway Experience. To Cathy Burns, Sharon Hargrave, Ginny Monk, Wib Newton, Sandra Perkins, Sherry Randolph, Todd Sandel, Carey Skinner, Nathan Phillips, Rajan Trafton, and Steve Trafton, we are grateful for the relationships and learning that have moved these ideas into print so others can benefit.

Terry Hargrave, Ph.D. is nationally recognized for his pioneering work with intergenerational families. Dr. Hargrave has authored numerous professional articles and eleven books including *Restoration Therapy: Understanding and Guiding Healing in Marriage and Family Therapy* (co-authored with Franz Pfitzer) and *The Essential Humility of Marriage: Honoring the Third Identity in Couple Therapy.*

Dr. Hargrave has presented nationally and internationally on the concepts and processes of family and marriage restoration, aging and is known for his clear and entertaining presentations. His work has been featured in several national magazines and newspapers, as well as ABC News 20/20, Good Morning America and CBS Early Morning. He has been selected as a national conference plenary speaker and as a Master's Series Therapist by the American Association for Marriage and Family Therapy.

He is a Professor of Marriage and Family Therapy at Fuller Seminary in Pasadena, California and is president and in practice at Amarillo Family Institute, Inc.

Shawn Stoever, Ph.D. received his doctoral degree in Counseling Psychology from the University of North Texas where he specialized in marriage and family therapy. He currently serves as a Senior Director for the WinShape Foundation (a non-profit ministry of Chick-fil-A) overseeing Marriage, Retreat, Experiential Learning ministries. Prior to his role at WinShape, Shawn served as the Director of Training for the Smalley Relationship Center, founded by Gary Smalley.

Shawn is passionate about his relationship with God and eager to share how you can experience fulfillment and joy in life. He is the co-author of the book, "The Wholehearted Marriage". Whether he's leading retreats, writing, or appearing on television and radio broadcasts, Shawn's humor, enthusiasm, and wisdom help him connect with his audience. Despite extensive schooling, Shawn really did not know anything about relationships until he met his wife Christina. They have four wonderful children, Taylor, Cade, Avery (with the Lord), and Cody.

FREE App
5 Days to a New Marriage

From the convenience of your smart phone, you can access tools and resources developed from the *5 Days to a New Marriage* book. You'll find information about marriage intensives, personalized therapist referrals, products, resources for increased insight, and content that works to reshape individuals and marriages.

Go to your App Store and enter New Marriage. It's a free download.

Download your 5 Days App today!